Grammar Wise 2

Kevin Anthony Keating

University of Arizona, Tucson

New Readers Press

Grammar Wise 2
ISBN 978-1-56420-431-8

Copyright © 2004 New Readers Press
New Readers Press
A Publishing Division of ProLiteracy
1320 Jamesville Avenue, Syracuse, New York 13210
www.newreaderspress.com

Printed in the United States of America
9 8 7 6 5 4 3

All proceeds from the sale of New Readers Press materials
support literacy programs in the United States and worldwide.

Acquisitions Editor: Paula L. Schlusberg
Content Editor: Judi Lauber
Production Manager: Andrea Woodbury
Designer: Andrea Woodbury
Illustrations: Kirsten Lindquist
Production Specialist: Jeffrey R. Smith
Cover Design: Andrea Woodbury

Contents

About This Book

Grammar Wise 2 is designed to teach basic grammar to high-beginning and low-intermediate ESL students. The text is appropriate for class use, homework, and independent study. The grammatical structures build progressively throughout the book, yet units are independent. Teachers can begin at any point, use the units in any order, and recycle topics or activities that students still need to master.

After reviewing parts of speech, sentence structure, and present-tense verbs, *Grammar Wise 2* covers count and noncount nouns, prepositions of time and place, object pronouns, comparative and superlative adjectives, and present progressive and past tenses. The final units deal with more complex structures: the definite article *the,* verb-plus-infinitive and verb-plus-gerund combinations, and the past progressive tense. Many exercises include questions and answers so that students can practice conversation and question formation.

Each unit of *Grammar Wise 2* focuses on a particular grammatical structure, but also recycles structures and vocabulary from earlier units. Each unit uses models, rather than formal rules, to introduce the target structure. Use the model sentences to draw attention to key features. Students can read and repeat the models and suggest other sentences that use the structure before moving on to the exercises.

The Grammar Handbook in Appendix 4 (pages 177–205) supplements these brief introductions for students who can can use more detailed explanations. The Handbook provides rules for each structure, including additional details of usage, common errors, and exceptions.

The exercises allow students to internalize new structures and contrast them with structures learned earlier. In each unit, exercises advance from recognition to production and from controlled answers to free expression. This progression helps students assimilate new material and move toward mastery. Units vary in length and in number of exercises, depending on the complexity of the target structure.

Similar kinds of exercises are repeated throughout the text. This repetition allows students to become familiar with what an exercise requires so that they can focus on the grammatical structure and can function more independently in class. Suggestions for conducting the activities, as well as specific suggestions for each unit, are presented in the *Grammar Wise Teacher's Guide.*

Dictation exercises in each unit provide a controlled aural introduction to the target structure. The sentences for dictation are provided in Appendix 3 (pages 170–176). Error-correction exercises help students develop editing skills. The items include the target structure, previously taught structures, and other structures familiar to students at this level. Many of these exercises also include one sentence with no errors.

Many exercises are followed by discussion questions related to topics or information from the exercise. These discussions can be whole-class activities, but they also provide excellent opportunities for students to practice natural conversation in pairs or small groups. The questions are designed to elicit structures and vocabulary from the exercise, personalizing the use of the structures by asking students about their own experience. At this level, some students may be able to produce only short, simple responses, while others will respond more elaborately. Encourage students to expand their answers and, when they talk with a partner, to ask for more details. Model and teach suitable follow-up questions.

Exercise items draw on topics relevant to students' lives and interests. Many relate to geography, nature, weather, history, and human behavior. Other items draw on students' experiences, for example, with food, sports, entertainment, work, and education. Some items ask about people in students' lives, such as their classmates, neighbors and friends, co-workers, and family members. If a student does not have the relative or person referred to, replace the term, or guide the student in adapting the response. For example, a student could say, "I don't have a brother," or tell about a different person: "I don't have a brother, but my sister has black hair."

Grammar Wise 2 is designed to take students beyond the mechanical study of grammar. It personalizes practice and helps students relate the material to their language needs outside class. The activities provide many opportunities to share personal information, encouraging meaningful interactions that promote both learning and natural language use.

Four Important Questions

A

What does "eraser" mean?

Meaning

What does _____ mean?
Example: What does "smile" mean?

Spelling

How do you spell _____?
Example: How do you spell "cough"?

Pronunciation

How do you pronounce _____?
Example: How do you pronounce "yawn"?

Translation

How do you say _____ in (language)?
Example: How do you say "yes" in Spanish?

Exercise 1: Meaning

Make questions about meaning. All the words name
parts of the body.

1. thumb: *What does "thumb" mean?*

2. toe: _____

3. knee: _____

4. elbow: _____

5. lip: _____

Discuss
a. What are the names of some other body parts?

Exercise 2: Spelling

Listen to the words the teacher reads. Ask how to spell them. Then
write questions. All the words are names of animals.

1. _____*whale*_____ : *How do you spell "whale"?*

2. _____ : _____

3. _____ : _____

4. _____ : _____

5. _____ : _____

Discuss
a. What are the names of some other animals?

Exercise 3: Pronunciation

Write questions about pronunciation. All the words name parts of a car.

1. tire: _How do you pronounce "tire"?_

2. horn: _____

3. engine: _____

4. windshield: _____

5. bumper: _____

Discuss

a. What are some other car parts?

Exercise 4: Translation

Write questions about translation.

1. thank you: _How do you say "thank you" in your language?_

2. hello: _____

3. very good: _____

4. money: _____

5. I love you: _____

Exercise 5

Choose words and write questions. Then ask your classmates.

1. meaning: _____

2. spelling: _____

3. pronunciation: _____

4. translation: _____

B Parts of Speech and Sentence Structure

He has a black cat in the box.

Nouns

A noun identifies something: a person, place, object, activity, emotion, etc.

Examples: Joseph, Mrs. Morrison, mother, boys, London, China, home, dog, flowers, car, coffee, music, swimming, soccer, reading, peace

Pronouns

A pronoun is a substitute for a noun.

Subject Pronouns

The subject pronouns are *I, you, we, he, she, it,* and *they.*

Examples: my son = he   you and I = we
           Kathy = she   two computers = they
           the weather = it

Adjectives

An adjective describes a noun.
Examples: big, cold, easy, fast, happy, interesting, red, tired

Adjectives and Nouns

Examples: I have a small dog.   (or)   My dog is small.
This is an interesting book.   (or)   This book is interesting.

Prepositions

Prepositions express the relationship of one noun to another.
They express place, time, direction, possession, etc.
Examples: in, at, on, to, from, for, of, near, with

Prepositional Phrases

Prepositional phrases are prepositions with nouns or noun phrases.
Examples: in the house, for you, at work, with my friend, on Tuesday

Verbs

There are two kinds of verbs: the verb *be*
and verbs that express actions.

The Verb *Be*

Present-tense forms of the verb *be* include *am, is,* and *are.*
Examples: I am a student.
The food is in the refrigerator.
My eyes are brown.

Other Verbs

Examples: eat, go, have, live, play, study, take, work

Sentences with Other Verbs

Examples: We eat dinner at 6:00 p.m.
He works every day.
I take a bus to school.

Sentence Structure: Noun or pronoun + *be* + noun

Examples: Jennifer is a police officer.
We are cousins.

Sentence Structure: Noun or pronoun + *be* + adjective

Examples: I am tired.
Those dogs are friendly.

Sentence Structure:
Noun or pronoun + *be* + prepositional phrase

Examples: I am at the mall.
Your book is on the table.

Sentence Structure: Noun or pronoun + verb + noun

Examples: We have class today.
Mark builds houses.

Sentence Structure:
Noun or pronoun + verb + prepositional phrase

Examples: I wake up at 6:00.
My neighbors come from Latvia.

Exercise 1: Dictation

Write the words that the teacher reads. Circle the part of speech.

1. _____they_____ : (noun (pronoun) adjective preposition verb *be* verb)

2. _____ : (noun pronoun adjective preposition verb *be* verb)

3. _____ : (noun pronoun adjective preposition verb *be* verb)

4. _____ : (noun pronoun adjective preposition verb *be* verb)

5. _____ : (noun pronoun adjective preposition verb *be* verb)

6. _____ : (noun pronoun adjective preposition verb *be* verb)

7. _____ : (noun pronoun adjective preposition verb *be* verb)

8. _____ : (noun pronoun adjective preposition verb *be* verb)

9. _____ : (noun pronoun adjective preposition verb *be* verb)

10. _____ : (noun pronoun adjective preposition verb *be* verb)

Exercise 2

Identify the parts of speech of the underlined words.

| noun | pronoun | adjective | preposition | verb *be* | other verb |

1. He swims <u>on</u> Saturdays. __preposition__

2. <u>We</u> listen to music at night. _____

3. She <u>studies</u> English. _____

4. <u>It</u> is cold today. _____

5. My television is <u>small</u>. _____

6. <u>Russian</u> is a difficult language. _____

7. Please come <u>with</u> me. _____

8. She <u>is</u> hungry. _____

9. He <u>swims</u> on Saturdays. _____

Discuss

a. **Is your class large or small?**
How many men and women are in the class?

b. **Where do you speak English?**

c. **What do you do in your free time?**

Exercise 3

Write two examples of each part of speech.

1. noun: __pencil, streets__

2. adjective: _____

3. verb *be*: _____

4. noun: _____

5. preposition: _____

6. verb: _____

7. pronoun: _____

Exercise 4

Write sentences. Put the words in order. Then write the parts of speech.

1. tall / Edward / is

   Edward is tall.

   Noun, verb be, adjective

2. lives / in an apartment / Derrick

   _____

   _____

3. strong / lions / animals / are

   _____

   _____

4. is / sweet / sugar

   _____

   _____

5. blue / has / Nancy / eyes

   _____

   _____

6. at the park / my children / are

   _____

   _____

7. a doctor / is / she

   _____

   _____

Present-Tense Verbs

He is not a good cook, so he often uses the microwave.

The Verb *Be*

Affirmative	Negative
He is a music teacher.	He isn't an engineer.
It's hot in the summer.	It is not cold in the summer.
My friends are at work.	They aren't at home.

Other Verbs

Affirmative	Negative
I like chicken and rice.	I don't like spicy food.
Alex lives in a small town.	He doesn't live in a big city.

There Is/There Are

Affirmative

There is a restaurant near here.

There are 16 students in our class.

Negative

There isn't a post office near here.

There aren't any Germans in our class.

Exercise 1: Dictation

Write the sentences that the teacher reads.

1. _____

2. _____

3. _____

4. _____

Discuss

a. What is another island?

b. What do you often eat for dinner?

c. Is there a bank near here?

d. What are some countries with a lot of oil?

Exercise 2

Circle the correct words.

1. (I (My name) (is) are) Alfredo.

2. I (tired am tired).

3. We (no are are no are not) (at on) the mall now.

4. (There is It is) (mailbox a mailbox the mailboxes)
   near (me my) house.

5. Most (people peoples) in my home country
   (no speak are not speak do not speak) English.

Discuss

a. How do you feel now?

b. Is there a mailbox near your home?

c. Do many people in your home country speak English?

Exercise 3

Fix any mistakes.

1. My friend ~~speak~~ *speaks* English well.

2. We usually hungry after class.

3. Eric don't walk to work. Drive his car.

4. Some peoples are exercise in morning.

5. It does not rain very much in the desert.

Discuss

a. Do you eat after class?
b. In your family, who drives to work?
c. Do you ever exercise? If yes, what kind of exercise do you do?
d. Does it rain much in your city?

Exercise 4

Write answers.

1. Question: Where are you from?

   Answer: I'm from Turkey.

2. Question: Where do you usually study?

   Answer: _____

3. Question: What time does your first class begin?

   Answer: _____

4. Question: How many women are there in your class?

   Answer: _____

5. Question: What color is your grammar book?

   Answer: _____

Exercise 5

Fill in the blanks. Add pronouns if necessary.

1. Jack _____*is*_____ (be) 26 _____*years*_____ (year) old.

2. Mario _____ (be not) in class today. _____ (be sick).

3. Muslims _____ (not drink) alcohol.

4. There _____ (be) 50 _____ (state) in the United States.

5. Today, a computer _____ (cost) about $1000.

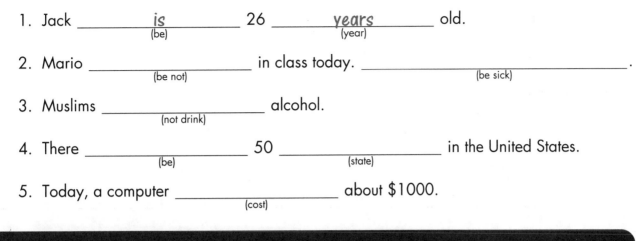

Discuss

a. Is anyone absent today? If yes, who?

b. What are some American states? What state do you live in?

c. Do you have a computer?

Exercise 6

Write sentences. Add and change words as necessary.

1. Russia / big country

   Russia is a big country.

2. our teacher / always / bring / book / class

   _____

3. lot / restaurant / have a no-smoking section

   _____

4. there / be / old university / Cambridge, England

   _____

5. people / not usually / wear / glove / in summer

   _____

Exercise 7

Write sentences. Use the words given, and add your own ideas.

1. my brother / have

   <u>My brother has two children.</u>

2. there is

   _____

3. there are not any

   _____

4. I do not

   _____

5. my friend does not

   _____

6. my teacher / be

   _____

7. people in the U.S. / be

   _____

8. today / it

   _____

9. my mother / have

   _____

10. my neighbors

    _____

11. my hair

    _____

B Present-Tense Questions

What time does your plane leave?

The Verb *Be*

Question	Answer
Are you tired today?	Yes, I am. (or) No, I'm not.
Is the class easy or difficult?	It's not easy, but I like it.
Where are your books?	They're on the desk.
Why is Janice absent today?	She's absent because she's sick.

Is There/Are There

Question	Answer
Is there a supermarket near here?	Yes, there is. (or) No, there isn't.
How many states are there in the U.S.?	There are 50 states in the U.S.

Other Verbs

Does he have a car?
Yes, he does.   (or)   No, he doesn't.

Do they speak Spanish or Portuguese in Brazil?
They speak Portuguese.

Who do you eat lunch with?
I usually eat lunch with my classmates.

Why does Claire get up so early?
She gets up early for work.

Some Question Words

how	when	which	whose
what	where	who	why

how far	how much	what color	what time
how many	how often	what kind	

Exercise 1: Dictation

Complete the questions that the teacher reads. Then write answers.
Discuss with a partner.

1. Question: _____ your best friend?

   Answer: _____

2. Question: _____ usually get up on weekdays?

   Answer: _____

3. Question: _____ talkative?

   Answer: _____

4. Question: _____ in your classroom?

   Answer: _____

5. Question: _____ a car?

   Answer: _____

Exercise 2

Circle the correct words. Write answers. Discuss with a partner.

1. Question: What street (is   do) you (live   lives) on?

   Answer: _____

2. Question: How far (is   are   does) your home from here?

   Answer: _____

3. Question: (Is   Are) there some (store   stores) near your home?

   Answer: _____

4. Question: (Is   Are   Do   Does) your home (has   have) a garage?

   Answer: _____

5. Question: How (much   many) people (live   are live) in your home?

   Answer: _____

Exercise 3

Fix any mistakes. Then write answers. Discuss with a partner.

1. Question: Where ~~are~~ *is* the bank?

   Answer: _The bank is on Park Avenue._____

2. Question: Are you have a bicycle?

   Answer: _____

3. Question: What kind of music do you listen to?

   Answer: _____

4. Question: Why you are here?

   Answer: _____

5. Question: There is an airport in your city?

   Answer: _____

Exercise 4

Complete the questions. Write answers. Discuss with a partner.

1. Where _____ *do you* _____ live?
   _(you)

   I live on the south side of town.

2. What room _____ your class in?
   _(be)

   _____

3. _____ friendly?
   _(people in your city / be)

   _____

4. Where _____ for food?
   _(you / shop)

   _____

5. In your home, who usually _____ dinner?
   _(cook)

   _____

Exercise 5

Read the answer. Then write the question.

1. Question: _*What time is the movie?*_____

   Answer: 8:00 p.m. The movie is at 8:00 p.m.

2. Question: _____

   Answer: Black. His hair is black.

3. Question: _____

   Answer: Juan's. It is Juan's book.

4. Question: _____

   Answer: $700. The TV costs $700.

5. Question: _____

   Answer: No. No, I don't like sushi.

Exercise 6

Complete the questions. Write answers. Discuss with a partner.

1. How _____ today?
   (you / feel)

   _____

2. _____ any American students in your class?
   (there / be)

   _____

3. _____ English well?
   (anyone in your family / speak)

   _____

4. Who _____ your class?
   (teach)

   _____

Exercise 7

Write your own questions and answers. Discuss with a partner.

1. How many . . . ?

   Question: _____

   Answer: _____

2. Is your home country . . . ?

   Question: _____

   Answer: _____

3. Do you . . . ?

   Question: _____

   Answer: _____

4. What time / you . . . ?

   Question: _____

   Answer: _____

Exercise 8: Dictation

Write the questions that the teacher reads. Write your answers.
Then share with a partner.

1. Question: _____

   Answer: _____

2. Question: _____

   Answer: _____

3. Question: _____

   Answer: _____

4. Question: _____

   Answer: _____

5. Question: _____

   Answer: _____

6. Question: _____ married or single?

   Answer: _____

7. Question: _____

   Answer: _____

8. Question: _____

   Answer: _____

9. Question: _____ studying English here?

   Answer: _____

10. Question: _____

    Answer: _____

1 Prepositions of Time

It is usually hot in the summer.

Some Prepositions of Time

at   during   in   on

Time Expressions with Prepositions

times: at 3:00, at 12:30 p.m.
days: on Saturday, on Saturdays (every Saturday), on Christmas
months: in January, in August
years: in 1995, in 1979
dates: on September 21, on April 16, 1951
seasons: in the winter, in the fall   (or)   in winter, in fall

More Time Expressions

Examples: on the first day, on Friday night
during the day, during the month
in the morning, in the evening
at noon, at night
on weekdays, on vacation
on the weekend   (or)   on weekends

Expressions without Prepositions

Examples: now
today
every day
last Monday
next week

Exercise 1: Dictation

Write the word that the teacher reads. Then write the word with a
preposition, if one is necessary.

	Time Word	Preposition
1.	afternoon	in the afternoon
2.		
3.		
4.		
5.		
6.		
7.		
8.		
9.		
10.		
11.		
12.		
13.		
14.		

Exercise 2

Circle the correct words.

1. We often (go goes) to the park (in at on) Sunday because we (have not do not have) class (in at on) the weekend.

2. (In At On) the summer, Maryanne (swim swims) (in at on) Mondays and Wednesdays.

3. Thanksgiving (no is is not) (in at on) December. It is (in at on) the fourth Thursday (in at on) November.

4. (In At On) midnight, (dark is dark it is dark) outside, so we cannot (to see see) very (good well).

5. In some cities, there (is not are not) many buses (in at during) night, and the streets (dangerous is dangerous are dangerous).

Exercise 3

Fix any mistakes.

1. Our class have homework every night, so we always are busy.

2. We pay rent on the first day of the month.

3. He always drink a glass of orange juice in morning.

4. There is many parties in December 31.

5. Some students no like classes early in morning.

6. There are 30 day on September.

Discuss

a. When do you do your homework?
b. Do you pay rent? If yes, when?
c. What do you drink in the morning?
d. When do you go to parties?
e. When do you like to have classes?
f. What month is it? How many days are there in this month?

Exercise 4

Complete the question and write the answer.

1. What time _____ on weekends?
   (you get up)

   _____

2. What day _____ shopping?
   (you often go)

   _____

3. When _____ a big holiday in your home country?
   (there)

   _____

4. What _____ the date today?
   (be)

   _____

Exercise 5

Write complete sentences. Keep the same word order.

1. many young people / go to a movie / Saturday

   _____

2. it / hot / summer in Texas

   _____

3. afternoon / my grandfather / always / take a nap

   _____

4. some people sleep / day / and work / night

   _____

Discuss

a. How often do you go to the movies?
   What kind of movies do you like?
b. In your home country, what is the weather like in the summer?
c. Do you take naps? If yes, when?

Exercise 6

Complete the sentences.

1. Many _____ _____ vacations
   (family)   (take)

   _____ because the weather
   (summer)

   _____ nice.
   (be)

2. In Europe, people often ski _____ because
   (winter)

   _____ a lot of snow.
   (there / be)

3. Students can travel _____
   (July)

   because their schools _____ closed.
   (be)

4. Elena _____ to a different place _____ .
   (go)   (every year)

5. _____ people
   (lot)

   _____
   (not cook)

   _____ .
   (vacation)

6. San Francisco and San Diego _____ popular
   (be)

   _____ to visit. _____ , restaurants
   (place)   (night)

   in _____
   (this city)

   _____ crowded.
   (be usually)

Discuss

a. When do you have a vacation?
b. What do you like to do in the summer?
c. Is there snow in your home country?
   If yes, what months have snow?
d. When are schools closed in your home country?
e. Do you usually cook on vacation?
f. What is another popular place to visit?

Exercise 7

Write sentences. Use the words given and add your ideas.

1. on the weekend / many students

   _____

2. on Friday / we

   _____

3. in the evening / my mother / usually

   _____

4. in the summer / people in my home country

   _____

5. every day / my teacher

   _____

6. at noon

   _____

7. my friend / often / at night

   _____

8. during the day

   _____

9. in the evening / I

   _____

10. on weekdays

   _____

11. on my birthday

   _____

2 Prepositions of Place

She lives in an apartment on Tenth Street.

Using Prepositions of Place

in: in California, in Thailand, in an apartment, in the newspaper,
     in the room
on: on the table, on Maple Street, on the radio, on TV
at: at 7725 Stone Street, at Symphony Hall, at the park,
     at a party, at home
to: go to school, come to my house

More Prepositions of Place

above	between	from	near	under
behind	close to	in back of	next to	
below	far from	in front of	over	

Examples: behind the supermarket = in back of the supermarket
          near Paris = close to Paris

Expressions without Prepositions

Examples: go home
sign here

Exercise 1: Dictation

Write the sentences that the teacher reads.

1. _____
2. _____
3. _____
4. _____
5. _____

Discuss

a. What page are we on?
b. Do you drive to school? If yes, where do you park?
c. Do you usually read the news? If yes, where?
d. Do you often use the Internet? If yes, where?

Exercise 2

Circle the correct words.

1. Please (sign to sign) your name (in on at) the line here and also
   (in at on) the back.

2. Some people (drink drinks) and (eat eats) a lot (in at on) parties.

3. Grandma sometimes (take takes) a nap (in at on) the afternoon
   (in at on) the sofa (in at on) the living room.

4. I (live lives) (in at on) (a an) apartment (in at on) the first floor
   (at under above) some very noisy (neighbor neighbors).

5. (Every day On every day), she (do does) her homework
   (the library at the library).

Exercise 3

Fix any mistakes.

1. There are malls at every big cities.

2. There are a shoe store next the music store.

3. I no go the mall on weekend because is crowded.

4. Karen works at a fast-food restaurant in the mall.

5. Meet me at 11:00 in front the south entrance. Don't late!

6. The parking lot at the mall often full, so we park far the entrance.

Discuss

a. Is there a mall in your city? Where is the mall?
b. How often do you go to the mall?
c. Do you have a favorite store? If yes, where is it?
d. Do you know people who work in stores? If yes, where?

Exercise 4

Complete the questions. Write answers. Discuss with a partner.

1. _____ any fast-food restaurants near school?
   (be there)

   _____

2. Who _____ next to in class?
   (you usually sit)

   _____

3. Where _____ the TV in your home?
   (be)

   _____

4. Where _____ carry their keys?
   (lot / woman)

   _____

Exercise 5

Complete the sentences.

1. Portugal _____ Spain.
   (be / next)

2. Baltimore _____ Washington, D.C.
   (be / not very far)

3. He _____ 8th Street.
   (not / live)

   His home _____ 2933 East Alta Street.
   (be)

4. _____ my party on Friday?
   (you / can come)

5. _____ always a lot of cars _____ my home.
   (there / be)   (front)

Discuss

a. Are you from the capital of your home country?
   If not, is your hometown far from the capital?
b. What is your address now?
c. Where do you go on weekends?

Exercise 6

Fill in the blanks. Use words from the list.

on	close to	in	below	above	between

1. The Nile River is _____ Egypt.

2. The United States is _____ Canada and Mexico.

3. New York City is _____ the East Coast of the U.S.

4. Seoul, South Korea, is _____ the border of North Korea.

5. The sky is _____ us; the earth is _____ us.

Discuss

a. Where is your home country? What countries border it?
b. Is there a big river in your home country? If yes, what is it?
c. Does your home country have a coast? If yes, what ocean?

Exercise 7

Write sentences. Add and change words as necessary.

1. Doug / park / his car / parking lot / behind his apartment

   _____

2. lot / people / go / beach or mountains / hot days

   _____

3. you / usually stay / home / the weekend?

   _____

4. I / always carry / cell phone / my backpack

   _____

Discuss

a. Where are the parking lots for your school?
b. What do you do on hot days?
c. Do you have a cell phone? If yes, where do you carry it?

Exercise 8

Write sentences with the words given and your ideas.

1. nobody lives

   _____

2. I often go to

   _____

3. in front of my home

   _____

4. not far from

   _____

Count and Noncount Nouns and Modifiers

There are many books here, but there is not much space.

Count and Noncount Nouns

There are two kinds of nouns in English: count nouns and noncount nouns.

Count Nouns

Count nouns have singular and plural forms. You can use specific numbers with count nouns.
Examples: 1 book—2 books—3 books
        a bird—some birds—a lot of birds

Noncount Nouns

Noncount nouns have only a singular form. You cannot use numbers with noncount nouns.
Examples: coffee—some coffee
        love—a lot of love

Some Types of Noncount Nouns

liquids:	water, milk
gases:	air, oxygen
emotions:	sadness, love
some kinds of food:	meat, bread
groups of things:	furniture, money
too many to count:	sand, snow
things you cannot touch:	time, music, information

Words to Use with Count Nouns

a   an   some   any   many   a lot of

Examples: a car
            some friends
            many students

Words to Use with Noncount Nouns

some   any   much   a lot of

Examples: some tea
            not much time
            a lot of money

With Questions and Negative Verbs

Examples: Do you have any brothers or sisters?
            She doesn't have much free time today.

Exercise 1: Dictation

Write the sentences that the teacher reads. Circle the nouns. Write *C*
for count nouns. Write *N* for noncount nouns.

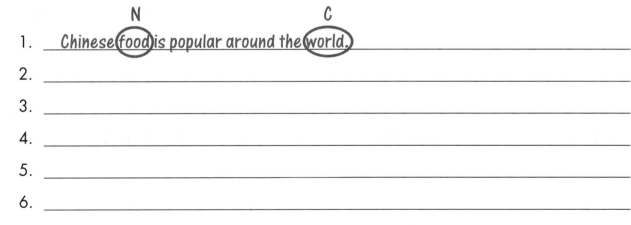

Exercise 2

Write the word *some* with each noun. Make the count nouns plural.
Don't change the noncount nouns.

1. apple: __some apples__

2. food: __some food__

3. pen: _____

4. homework: _____

5. music: _____

6. song: _____

7. liter: _____

8. gas: _____

9. ring: _____

10. jewelry: _____

11. work: _____

12. job: _____

13. news: _____

14. word: _____

15. vocabulary: _____

16. child: _____

Exercise 3

Circle the correct words.

1. Hindus never (eat   eats   eat a) meat.

2. Our team (needs   is need   need) (a   some) luck to win.

3. (In   At   On) winter, there (is a   are a   is   are) snow (in   at) Vermont.

4. Please give me (an   some) (advice   advices).

5. (Are we   Do we) have (a   any) milk?

6. There (is not   no is   are not) (much   many) good news (on   in) TV.

Exercise 4

Write sentences. Add and change words as necessary.

1. _____
   (my friend's / vocabulary / very large)

   _____
   (every day / she / learn / 10 new word)

2. _____
   (there / not any furniture / this room)

   _____
   (we need / chair / table)

3. _____
   (German beer / famous)

   _____
   (German people / lot / beer)

4. _____
   (there / not much peace / the world today)

   _____
   (news / TV / usually / bad)

5. _____
   (Dan / have / about 50 shirt)

   _____
   (spend / lot / money on / clothes)

6. _____
   (Los Angeles / have / lot / pollution)

   _____
   (there / many car / but not / any subway)

7. _____
   (people / Japan / lot / rice and fish)

   _____
   (also / eat / many other kind / food)

Discuss

a. Do you have a large vocabulary? How do you learn new words?
b. How much furniture is there in your home?
c. Do you spend a little or a lot of money on clothes?
d. Do people in your home country drink beer? What do they drink?
e. Are there any subways in your city?
f. What kinds of food are popular in your home country?

Exercise 5

Complete the questions. Write answers. Discuss with a partner.

1. How often _____ ?
   (you eat / fast food)

   _____

2. What restaurant _____ ?
   (sell / good sandwich)

   _____

3. Do you _____ ?
   (wear / much jewelry)

   _____

4. Does anyone in your family _____ ?
   (wear / earring)

   _____

5. What color _____ ?
   (be / your mother's eye)

   _____

6. What color _____ ?
   (be / her hair)

   _____

7. _____ easy or difficult for you?
   (be / English grammar)

   _____

8. _____ ?
   (you / understand / count and noncount noun)

   _____

9. _____ in your home?
   (be there / air conditioning)

   _____

10. Do you _____ ?
    (have / garden)

    _____

11. When _____ ?
    (you have / free time)

    _____

12. How many _____ ?
    (time / a week / you / eat out)

    _____

Exercise 6

Fix any mistakes.

1. Some students are have a lot of homeworks.

2. I listen a music every day.

3. Please open window. This room needs air.

4. My father always puts some sugar in his tea.

5. I can't to sleep if there is too many noise.

6. Every country wants a peace.

7. Are you like cold weather? No, I no like a cold weather.

8. He don't have much money.

Discuss

a. What music do you like? How many music CDs do you have?
b. Do you drink tea? What do you like in your tea?
c. Is your home quiet or noisy? How many people live there?
d. What is the money in your home country?
e. What kind of weather do you like?

Exercise 7

Complete the sentences. Use the names of people you know.

1. _____ _____ any _____ .
   (not have)   (child)

2. _____ _____ some _____ .
   (have)   (photograph)

3. Where _____ lives, there _____ much
                     (be not)
   _____ .
   (snow)

4. _____ _____ a lot of _____ .
   (wear)   (makeup)

5. _____ _____ many _____ of
   (like)   (kind)
   _____ .
   (music)

Exercise 8

Write sentences with the words.

1. news

   _____

2. keys

   _____

3. orange juice

   _____

4. gas

   _____

5. museum

   _____

6. ice

   _____

7. health

   _____

8. bus

   _____

9. cup of coffee

   _____

10. questions

    _____

4 Object Pronouns

He loves her, and she loves him.

Pronouns

Pronouns substitute for nouns.
Example: John reads the newspaper. = He reads the newspaper.

Forms of Pronouns

Subject Pronouns		Object Pronouns	
I	we	me	us
you	you	you	you
he/she/it	they	him/her/it	them

Using Object Pronouns

Object pronouns come after a verb or a preposition.
Examples: I call my mother on Tuesdays. = I call her on Tuesdays.
Amy always listens to her parents. = She always listens to them.
My dad lives near me, so I see him often.

Exercise 1: Dictation

Write the sentences that the teacher reads.

1. <u>Donald loves Susanna.</u>

   <u>Donald loves her.</u>

2. _____

   _____

3. _____

   _____

4. _____

   _____

5. _____

   _____

Exercise 2

Change all of the nouns in Exercise 1 to pronouns.

1. <u>He loves her.</u>

2. _____

3. _____

4. _____

5. _____

Discuss

a. Where do you keep your books?

b. Do you have any children? Where are they now?

c. Who usually sits next to you?

d. How well do you know your neighbors? Do you talk often?

Exercise 3

Circle the correct words.

1. Many (people   peoples) (wear   wears   are wear) glasses.
   (They   Them) need (it   they   them) because (their   them) eyes
   (are not   do not) strong.

2. Every day, the teacher (explain   explains) the grammar to (we   us),
   but sometimes we (aren't   don't) understand (he   she   him   her).

3. Please (come   comes) with (I   me). (I   Me) (has   have) a problem,
   and (I   me) need (you   your) help.

4. Mrs. Freeman (like   likes) to talk. (She   Her) (live   lives) alone, so
   (I   me) call (he   she   him   her) every week.

5. Mr. Franco (live   lives) near (I   me). (His   He) wife's name (is   are)
   Albertina, but (he   him) always calls (she   her) "Honey."

Discuss

a. Do you wear glasses? When?
b. Do you like grammar? Do you usually understand the grammar?
c. If you have a problem, who helps you?
d. Who do you phone a lot? When do you usually call them?
e. Do you call anyone "Honey"? Who calls you "Honey"?

Exercise 4

Fix any mistakes.

1. Spelling is not easy. The teacher often spells the words for us.

2. Many people are love blue jeans. They wear it almost every day.

3. Edward need some money. Please give some money to her.

4. That used computer is not work very well. Don't buy him.

5. Jeff really like his girlfriend Eva. He call them every night.

6. The buses in this town often late. We wait a long time for they.

Exercise 5

Write pairs of sentences. Use pronouns in the second part.

1. _Mr. Green loves rice._
   (Mr. Green / love / rice)
   He often eats it for dinner.
   (often / eat / dinner)

2. _____
   (Sandra / not have / car)
   _____
   (her mother / bring / school / every day)

3. _____
   (Theresa's father / be / sick)
   _____
   (she / visit / every weekend)

4. _____
   (sometimes / I / forget / homework)
   _____
   (leave / home)

5. _____
   (Japanese students / take / many test)
   _____
   (must take / in high school)

6. _____
   (teacher / go / out with my classmates and me)
   _____
   (drink coffee with)

7. _____
   (my classmates and I / watch / English videos)
   _____
   (help / learn English)

8. _____
   (I / always / listen / my father)
   _____
   (respect)

Discuss

a. Is anyone in your family sick now? Do you visit him/her?
b. How often do you forget your homework?
c. How often do you have tests? Do you like tests?
d. Do you like coffee? Do you ever drink coffee with your teacher?
e. Do you watch videos in English or in your first language? Why?
f. Who do you always listen to? Why?

Exercise 6

Complete the first sentence. Use the names of people you know.
Then, write the sentence again with pronouns and a reason.

1. I often talk to _____ Maria _____ .

   I talk to her _____

   because _she is interesting_ _____ .

2. I sometimes study with _____ .

   _____

   because _____ .

3. _____ sits between _____ and

   _____ .

   _____

   because _____ .

4. _____ sometimes helps me.

   _____

   because _____ .

5. After class, the teacher often talks to _____ and

   _____ .

   _____

   because _____ .

6. _____ sometimes smiles at _____ .

   _____

   because _____ .

7. _____ sometimes uses my eraser.

   _____

   because _____ .

Exercise 7

Complete the questions. Add any necessary words. Write answers using pronouns and your ideas. Then discuss with a partner.

1. Where _do you keep_ _____ the ice cream?
   (you keep)

   I keep it in the freezer. _____

2. Where _____ their money?
   (people often put)

   _____

3. When _____ your family?
   (you call)

   _____

4. What _____ your teacher about?
   (the class / often ask)

   _____

5. What _____ you and your classmates?
   (the teacher often give)

   _____

6. Where _____ shoes?
   (you buy)

   _____

5 Comparative and Superlative Adjectives

A car is faster and more expensive than a bicycle.

Comparative Adjectives

The comparative forms of adjectives compare two things.
Use *than* before the second noun.
Examples: Egypt is an older country than Canada.
I think action movies are more interesting than romantic comedies.

Superlative Adjectives

The superlative forms of adjectives compare more than two things.
Use *the* before the superlative form.
Examples: She is the youngest student in the class.
They live in the most expensive house on the street.

Forms with Short Words

In general, use *-er* and *-est* with words that have one or two syllables.
If the word ends with a vowel + consonant, double the consonant.

Adjective	Comparative	Superlative
small	smaller	the smallest
large	larger	the largest
big	bigger	the biggest
weak	weaker	the weakest

Examples: A mouse is smaller than a cat.
An elephant is the biggest animal in Africa.

Forms with Long Words

Use *more* and *most* with some words, especially words that have more than two syllables.

Adjective	Comparative	Superlative
common	more common	the most common
difficult	more difficult	the most difficult
interesting	more interesting	the most interesting

Examples: My name is more common than your name.
For me, math is the most difficult subject.

Forms of Words Ending in *y*

Adjective	Comparative	Superlative
easy	easier	the easiest
busy	busier	the busiest

Examples: For some students, English is easier than math.
For many people, Monday is the busiest day of the week.

Forms of Irregular Adjectives

Adjective	Comparative	Superlative
good	better	the best
bad	worse	the worst
far	farther	the farthest

Examples: This year's team is better than last year's.
His health today is worse than five years ago.
Which Central American country is the farthest south?

Exercise 1: Dictation

The teacher will dictate some adjectives. Write each adjective.
Then write the forms.

	Adjective	Comparative	Superlative
1.	big	bigger	the biggest
2.			
3.			
4.			
5.			
6.			
7.			
8.			
9.			
10.			

Exercise 2

Circle the correct words.

1. For me, English is (difficult   more difficult) (than   that) my first language.

2. (Is   Are) dogs (good   better   more better) pets (than   then) cats?

3. Portugal is (small than   more smaller than   smaller than) Brazil.

4. Is a snail (more slow   slower   the slowest) animal in the world?

5. An ocean is (salty   saltier   more saltier) (than   then) a river.

6. For girls (in   on   at) Mexico, the 15th birthday is
(more   most   the more   the most) important birthday.

Discuss
a. What languages do you speak? Which is the most difficult?
b. Is your home country bigger or smaller than the countries near it?
c. In your home country, which birthday is the most important?

Exercise 3

Complete the question. Write an answer that uses the comparative or superlative adjective. Then discuss with a partner.

1. Which animal is _____ (fast) _____, a horse or a cow?

   _____

2. What is _____ (fast) _____ animal in the world?

   _____

3. On TV, which sport is _____ (popular) _____, tennis or volleyball?

   _____

4. What is _____ (popular) _____ sport in your home country?

   _____

5. For you, which subject is _____ (easy) _____, math or English?

   _____

6. For you, what is _____ (easy) _____ subject in school?

   _____

7. Which country is _____ (big) _____, China or Egypt?

   _____

8. What is _____ (big) _____ country in the world?

   _____

9. What is _____ (large) _____ city in your home country?

   _____

10. Which do you like _____ (good) _____—chicken or fish?

   _____

11. Which do you like _____ (good) _____—Japanese food, Chinese food, or Italian food?

   _____

Exercise 4

Fix any mistakes.

1. Politics is more interesting sports.

2. Smith and Jones is the most common English names.

3. Usually, women have longer hair than men.

4. A whale is bigest animal the world.

5. An elephant is heavyest land animal.

6. Sugar is the baddest thing for your teeth.

7. Fresh fruit is more better that canned fruit.

8. Mount Everest more high than Mount Fuji.

9. Kuwait is far north than Oman.

> ### Discuss
> a. Are you more interested in politics or sports?
> b. What is the most common name in your home country?
> c. In your class, whose hair is longest? Shortest? Curliest? Darkest?
> d. Which U.S. state is the farthest north?

Exercise 5

Complete the sentences. Use the names of people in your class.

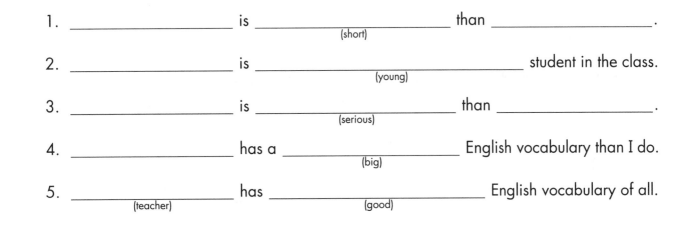

1. _____ is _____ than _____ .
   (short)

2. _____ is _____ student in the class.
   (young)

3. _____ is _____ than _____ .
   (serious)

4. _____ has a _____ English vocabulary than I do.
   (big)

5. _____ has _____ English vocabulary of all.
   (teacher)   (good)

Exercise 6

Write sentences. Use comparative or superlative adjectives.

1. buses / big / cars

   _____

2. the "Bullet Train" / fast train / Japan

   _____

3. in some city / bicycles / common / cars

   _____

4. Dave motorcycle / noisy / my motorcycle

   _____

5. O'Hare Airport / Chicago / busy airport / United States

   _____

Exercise 7

Write sentences with the words.

1. the best

   _____

2. slower

   _____

3. the most quiet

   _____

4. more dangerous

   _____

5. cheapest

   _____

6 Modals: *Can, Might, Should, Must*

She can play the violin very well.

Meaning

can = ability or permission
might = possibility; maybe
should = advice
must = necessity; obligation
must not = prohibition

Examples: Johannes is from Germany. He can speak German.
I am not sure, but it might rain tomorrow.
You are tired. You should go to bed.
You must not drink and drive! It is dangerous.

Structure: Modal + Verb

Examples: She can play basketball very well.
It might be windy tomorrow.

Negative: Modal + *not* + Verb

Examples: He cannot speak English.   (or)   He can't speak English.
You must not forget.

Questions: Modal + Subject + Verb

Examples: Can you help me?
Where might you go on vacation?
What should you not eat?   (or)   What shouldn't you eat?

Exercise 1: Dictation

Write the sentences that the teacher reads.

1. _____

2. _____

3. _____

4. _____

Discuss

a. What should parents teach their children?
b. Can many people in your home country speak English?

Exercise 2

Circle the correct words.

1. He (not rich   isn't rich   no is rich), so he (can   can't)
   (buy   buys   to buy) a new car. He (must buy   buys   to buy) a used car.

2. I (am not   do not) sure, but I (might   must) go (to   in)
   the mountains tomorrow. (You can   Can you) (go   to go) with (I   me)?

3. During a test, students (must   no must   must not) look at another
   (student   students   student's) paper. They must (keep   to keep)
   their eyes (in   on) their own papers.

4. Teachers (should be   should) on time for class.
   (He   They) should not (be   to be) late.

5. You (can't   shouldn't) (talk   to talk) a lot in (library   a library).
   Libraries should be (quiet   quiets) places.

Exercise 3

Complete the questions. Write answers. Discuss with a partner.

1. What _____ (you can do) very well?

   _____

2. What _____ (you can't do) very well?

   _____

3. If you are sick, what _____ (you should do) ?

   _____

4. If you are sick, what _____ (you should not do) ?

   _____

5. If you drive too fast, what might _____ (happen) ?

   _____

6. If you _____ (not study) , what might happen?

   _____

7. What must good workers _____ (do) ?

   _____

8. What must children _____ (not do) ?

   _____

9. What country might _____ (win) the next World Cup in soccer?

   _____

Exercise 4

Fix any mistakes.

1. He can't to buy beer. He too young.

2. Our car is really dirty. We might to wash him tomorrow.

3. I need help! Why you can't help me?

4. You must always wear a seatbelt in the car.

5. Good grades is important. You should be study.

Exercise 5

Write pairs of sentences. Add and change words as necessary.

1. _____
   (Maria / sick)

   _____
   (might / absent / tomorrow)

2. _____
   (today / very cold)

   _____
   (shouldn't / wear shorts)

3. _____
   (that girl / 14 years old)

   _____
   (cannot / a driver's license yet)

4. _____
   (our tests / always / difficult)

   _____
   (I / might not / an A)

5. _____
   (can't / my car / to school)

   _____
   (must / the bus)

6. _____
   (people in a theater / should / quiet)

   _____
   (should not / during the show)

Exercise 6

Write sentences or questions. Add and change words as necessary.

1. Anna's mother / from / France, / but Anna / cannot / French

   _____

2. David / cannot / find / key, / so / cannot / door

   _____

3. I / should / bring / jacket? / yes, it / might / cold

   _____

4. Ellen / should / not / swim / because / sick

   _____

5. police officers / should never / money from people

   _____

6. tomorrow's test / important, / so / tonight / we / must

   _____

7. the boy / should / his hands / before / dinner

   _____

8. the meeting / begin / 2:00. / we / must not / late!

   _____

9. I / might not / time / for lunch today

   _____

10. you / tired. / you / should / bed.

   _____

Discuss

a. What keys do you have? Can you always find them?
b. Do you usually eat breakfast? What might you eat for breakfast?
c. Are you tired? Should you go to bed early tonight?

Exercise 7

Write pairs of sentences. Start with the names of people you know.
Use the words below the line.

1. _____
   (often sick)

   _____
   (should)

2. _____
   (drives really fast)

   _____
   (might)

3. _____
   (want to learn English)

   _____
   (should not)

4. _____
   (be too young)

   _____
   (cannot)

5. _____
   (smoke a lot)

   _____
   (might)

6. _____
   (has an important meeting)

   _____
   (must not)

7. _____
   (know how to cook)

   _____
   (should)

8. _____
   (not have much money)

   _____
   (cannot)

9. _____
   (wants a new job)

   _____
   (must)

7 Adverbs

She runs quickly.

Adjectives and Adverbs

Adjectives describe nouns. They may be used with the verb *be*.
Adverbs usually modify verbs.

Adjective + noun	**Verb + adverb**
He is a quiet man.	He speaks quietly.
They hire safe drivers.	Some people don't drive safely.
This singer is good.	She sings well.

Regular and Irregular Adverbs

Many adverbs end with *-ly*. Some adverbs are irregular.

Adjective	**Adverb**
slow	slowly
easy	easily
good	well
fast	fast

Exercise 1: Dictation

Write the word the teacher reads. Identify the word by circling *adjective* or *adverb*.

1. _____ : (adjective   adverb)

2. _____ : (adjective   adverb)

3. _____ : (adjective   adverb)

4. _____ : (adjective   adverb)

5. _____ : (adjective   adverb)

6. _____ : (adjective   adverb)

7. _____ : (adjective   adverb)

8. _____ : (adjective   adverb)

9. _____ : (adjective   adverb)

Exercise 2

Circle the correct words.

1. Please (speak   to speak) (quiet   quietly). The baby (is   are) asleep
   (in   at   on) the bedroom.

2. At work, employees are sometimes (tired   tiredly). They
   (no do   do not do) their work very (good   well).

3. Some tests (is not   are not   no are) (difficult   difficultly).
   Students can (answer   answers) the questions (easy   easily).

4. If you have a (serious   seriously) problem, you should
   (talk   to talk) (private   privately) with the teacher.

5. In (cities big   big cities), traffic (is   are) often (heavy   heavily).
   People can't (drive   to drive) (fast   fastly).

Exercise 3

Fix any mistakes.

1. A baby's skin is softly.

2. She kisses her baby softly.

3. People must be quietly in a theater or concert hall.

4. We have to eat quick, or we might late for the movie.

5. You always are lately for class. Why you don't wake up more earlier?

6. The roads wet. We should drive careful.

Discuss

a. Is there a baby in your family? How should you hold a baby?
b. Do you eat quickly or slowly?
c. When do you like to wake up?
d. What are some things careful drivers do?

Exercise 4

Put the words in order. Write the sentences.

1. play / some / well / soccer / people

   _____

2. questions / students / incorrectly / sometimes / answer

   _____

3. grandmother / to / early / my / bed / goes

   _____

4. speaks / always / fast / he

   _____

5. never / I / completely / him / understand

   _____

Exercise 5

Fill in the blanks. Add any necessary words.

1. Francesca usually _____ all of the _____
   (answer)   (question)
   _____, so she _____ As on her quizzes.
   (correct)   (get)

2. Sometimes, I wake up _____, so I _____
                          (late)   (not have)
   time for breakfast. I _____ _____ to work.
                          (go)   (direct)

3. Your mother _____ very _____. Her meals
                (cook)   (good)
   _____ delicious.
   (always)

4. On the autobahn in Germany, no one _____
                                        (drive)
   _____. It's _____ road.
   (slow)   (dangerous)

5. A 16-year-old cannot _____ cigarettes _____ in
                          (buy)   (legal)
   the United States. People must _____ 18 to buy them.
                                    (be)

Discuss

a. In your family, who cooks well?
b. Do people in your home country drive fast? Are the roads safe?
c. How old must a person be to buy cigarettes in your home country?

Exercise 6

Write pairs of sentences.

1. _____
   (he / often sick)
   _____
   (he / go / the doctor / frequent)

2. _____
   (that football team / very good)
   _____
   (always / win / games / easy)

3. _____
   (today / we / not have / enough time)
   _____
   (we / can't finish / our work / complete)

Exercise 7

Write sentences about Karen, a bank teller.

1. Karen / do / her job / good

   _____

2. she / count / money / careful

   _____

3. all of the teller / polite / helpful

   _____

4. sometimes / the bank / very busy

   _____

5. usually / the customers / wait / patient

   _____

6. Karen / work / hard, but / like / job

   _____

Exercise 8

Complete the sentences. Use the names of classmates.

1. _____ _____ in class.
   (be / quiet)

2. _____ _____.
   (speak / soft)

3. _____ and _____ speak English very

   _____.
   (good)

4. _____ _____ student.
   (be / serious)

5. _____ _____.
   (study / hard)

6. _____ _____ class _____.
   (attend)   (regular)

Exercise 9

Write sentences with the words.

1. quickly

_____

_____

2. safely

_____

_____

3. strong

_____

_____

4. well

_____

_____

5. quietly

_____

_____

6. hard

_____

_____

7. carefully

_____

_____

8 Present Progressive Tense

They are watching TV now.

Meaning

Simple present tense = usually, always, every day, never
Present progressive tense = right now, at this time, this week, this year

Simple Present	**Present Progressive**
We study every day.	We are studying right now.
We always speak English in class.	The teacher is speaking English now.

Form

Present progressive form = verb *be* + (verb + *-ing*)
Example: I am listening to the teacher now.
Incorrect: ~~He is sleep right now.~~
Correct: He is sleeping right now.

Negatives

Present progressive negative = verb *be* + *not* + (verb + *-ing*)
Example: I am not listening to music now.

Questions

Present progressive question = verb *be* + subject + (verb + *-ing*)
Examples: Are you listening to me?
        What is he doing?

Exceptions

Some verbs normally use the simple present form only. These verbs
include *believe, forget, have, like, love, need, remember,
understand,* and *want.*
Examples: I understand you now.
        She does not love me now.
        What do you want?

More Exceptions

The verbs *live* and *feel* may occur in either simple present or
present progressive form, with no change in meaning:
Example: They live in Tokyo now. = They're living in Tokyo now.
        I don't feel well. = I'm not feeling well.

Exercise 1: Dictation

**Write the sentences that the teacher reads. Circle and say the verbs.
Are they in the simple present or the present progressive?**

1. _____

2. _____

3. _____

4. _____

5. _____

6. _____

Exercise 2

**Look at the pictures. Write sentences that tell what is happening.
Use the present progressive tense.**

1. The woman ___is riding a horse___ .

2. The horse _____ .

3. People _____ .

4. They _____ .

5. The children _____ .

6. They _____ .

7. The driver _____ .

8. The dog _____ .

9. The man _____ .

10. His radio _____ .

11. The sun _____ .

12. Birds _____ .

Exercise 3

Circle the correct words.

1. Every day, my brother (watch   watches   is watching) sports on TV,
   but right now he (watches   watching   is watching) the news.

2. It often (snows   snow   is snowing) (in   at   on) Canada (in   at   on)
   winter, but right now it (not snow   is not snowing).

3. (In   At) Caracas, José (live   lives   living) with his parents, but now
   he (living   live   is living) alone in (a   an) apartment (in   on) Miami.

4. Eddie usually (practice   is practicing   practices) guitar every
   afternoon. He (gets   is getting   is get) pretty good now.

5. We (goes   is going   are going) (in   to   at) class today, but (in   at   on)
   the weekend we (not have   not having   do not have) class.

6. Mrs. Harris (try   trying   is trying) to lose some (weight   weights).
   (He   She) (want   wants   is wanting) to be (health   healthier).

7. My neighbors (paint   are paint   are painting) (his   their   its)
   house this week. It (not   isn't   no is) easy work!

Discuss

a. Do you watch the news on TV?
b. Is there much snow in your home country?
c. Do you play a musical instrument?
d. How many days do you have class each week?
e. Do you exercise a lot?
f. What color is your home?

Exercise 4

Write sentences about what is happening around you right now.

1. _Mohammed and Julia are talking to each other._
2. _____
3. _____
4. _____
5. _____
6. _____

Exercise 5

Complete the sentences truthfully. Use negatives as needed. Then discuss with a partner.

1. Right now, the teacher _____ .
   (sit down)

   He/she _____ .
   (stand)

2. I never _____ _____ shoes.
   (wear)   (color)

   At this moment, I _____ _____ shoes.
   (wear)   (color)

3. _____ a lot in this city.
   (rain)

   Right now, _____ .
   (rain)

4. Today, we _____ noncount nouns.
   (study)

   We _____ the present progressive tense.
   (study)

5. Right now, I _____ for food.
   (shop)

   I usually _____ for food on _____ .
   (shop)

Exercise 6

Complete the question and write the answer. Discuss with a partner.

1. _____ right now?
   (anyone in class / laugh)

   _____

2. What color eyes _____ ?
   (your best friend / have)

   _____

3. _____ about right now?
   (your teacher probably think)

   _____

4. _____ gum right now?
   (any student / chew)

   _____

5. _____ a vacation?
   (you plan)

   _____

Exercise 7

Fix any mistakes.

1. Our teacher speak two language. right now is speaking English.

2. Usually, I sitting next to the window. I am like to look outside.

3. My mother's eyes is very good, so she is not needing glasses.

4. Many countries is changing very quick nowadays.

5. This year, my brothers are learning about computers.

6. My classmates are do his homework now.

7. In today, the sun is not shine.

8. Some students are always come late in class.

9. I hungry. I thinking about food now.

Exercise 8

Write sentences. Add and change words as necessary.

1. there / some problem / world / today

   _____

2. several / country / fight / war / now

   _____

3. at this moment / lot / company / cut / tree / rain forest

   _____

4. in some country / child / starve / right now

   _____

5. people / many city / not have / jobs / today

   _____

Exercise 9

Write about famous people. Use your imagination.

1. Who is a famous businessperson? _____ Bill Gates _____

   What is he/she probably doing right now? __He is probably working in his office.__

   _____

2. Who are two famous athletes? _____ and _____

   What are they probably doing right now? _____

   _____

3. Who is a famous actor? _____

   What is he/she probably doing right now? _____

   _____

4. Who is the leader of your home country? _____

   What is he/she probably doing right now? _____

   _____

5. Who are two famous singers? _____ and _____

   What are they probably doing right now? _____

   _____

6. Who is the president of the United States? _____

   What is he/she probably doing right now? _____

   _____

Future Tense

It's going to rain this weekend, and it will be very cold.

Two Forms to Express the Future

will + verb
be + *going to* + verb
Examples: Tomorrow, the race will start at 8:00 a.m.
He is going to graduate next year.

Will + Verb

Examples: I will call you tonight.
She'll help me.

Will + Verb *Be* + Adjective or Preposition

Examples: It will be cold tomorrow.
Next year, I'll be in Europe.

Be + Going to + Verb

Examples: I am going to finish tomorrow.
My sister is going to finish next week.

Questions with Future Tense

Examples: When will the program finish?
Will it be hot tomorrow?
Are you going to get up early tomorrow?
Where is the party going to be?

Negatives with Future Tense

Examples: You will not (won't) need any money at the show tonight.
He is not going to come next week.

Contractions

Examples: I will = I'll
they will = they'll
will not = won't

Phrases That Express the Future

next _____ : They will return to their country next month.
in _____ :   It is going to begin in 15 minutes.
this _____ :   I'm not going to move this weekend.
soon: We'll decide soon.
tomorrow: Are you going to go out tomorrow night?
tonight: What are you going to do tonight?

Exercise 1: Dictation

Write the sentences that the teacher reads.

1. _____

2. _____

3. _____

4. _____

5. _____

6. _____

Exercise 2

Circle the correct words.

1. The bank (not be open   won't be open) (next   on next) Monday. (Is   He is   It is) a holiday.

2. (Next week   The next week), the test (is difficult   will be difficult), so my classmate and I (going to study   am going to study   are going to study) together (this weekend   on this weekend).

3. I (sure   am sure) the teacher (will not late   will not be late   won't late) tomorrow. Our teacher (never late   is never late).

4. (We   Our) apartment (small   is small), so next month we (will going   are going) to look for a (more big   bigger   more bigger) place.

Discuss

a. Do you know anyone who is going to have a baby? When?
b. What is the next holiday? When will it be?
c. When is your next test? When will you study?
d. Is your home large or small? Are you going to move soon?

Exercise 3

Fix any mistakes.

1. If you drive too fastly, you will to have an accident.

2. The English course will end on three week.

3. What country going to winning the next soccer World Cup?

4. After class, some of my classmate will probably be go out for coffee.

5. I am no going to study on tonight.

6. We're going to get up early tomorrow morning.

Exercise 4

Complete the questions and write answers. Discuss with a partner.

1. _____ to your home country soon?
   (you / going / return)

   _____

2. What time _____ tonight?
   (you / will get home)

   _____

3. When _____ you?
   (your friends / going / visit)

   _____

4. When _____ your family again?
   (you / going / talk)

   _____

5. How long _____ this city?
   (you / going / stay)

   _____

6. Where _____ in 5 years?
   (you / will be)

   _____

7. _____ anything this weekend?
   (you / going / buy)

   _____

Exercise 5

What are you going to do this weekend? Write sentences. Then discuss with a partner.

1. _This weekend I will cut the grass._

2. _I'm going to make soup on Sunday._

3. _____

4. _____

5. _____

6. _____

7. _____

Exercise 6

Fill in the blanks. Add any necessary words.

1. The car _____ flat tire, but it _____ and
   (have)   (dark)

   I can't _____ very _____.
           (see)   (good)

   I _____ tomorrow.
     (fix)

2. Hurry up! We _____.
                 (late)

   _____ soon?
   (you / ready)

3. You _____ today,
       (might / sad)

   but tomorrow you _____ better.
                    (feel)

4. Tomorrow, we _____ the zoo.
                (visit)

   I _____ my camera.
     (bring)

5. She _____ tennis. Tomorrow, the match _____ TV,
       (love)   (be)

   so she _____ home and _____ it.
          (stay)   (watch)

6. Let's _____ the museum tomorrow.
         (go)

   It _____.
      (interesting and fun)

7. He _____ his daughter to school now,
      (take)

   but he _____ hour.
          (back)

Exercise 7

Make predictions. Write sentences about these topics.

1. your job in the future

   In the future, I will be an engineer.

2. your country in 10 years

   In 10 years, my country is going to use more solar energy.

3. your job in the future

   In the future, _____.

4. your country in 10 years

   In 10 years, _____.

5. your friend next year

   Next year, _____.

6. your grade on the next test

   On the next test, _____.

7. cars in 20 years

   In 20 years, _____.

8. the United States in 50 years

   In 50 years, _____.

9. your teacher in 15 years

   In 15 years, _____.

10. families in the 22nd century

    In the 22nd century, _____.

11. computers in the future

    In the future, _____.

Write sentences.

1. tonight / we / going / watch / weather report / TV

   _____

2. tomorrow / will / cold, so I / wear / warm jacket and glove

   _____

3. going / sunny but cold / this afternoon

   _____

4. not going / rain tomorrow / so / we / not / need / umbrella

   _____

5. tomorrow / going / windy. / it / perfect weather for kites

   _____

6. we / going / have / storm. / there / be / lot of snow

   _____

7. my neighbors / probably / spend next winter / Florida

   _____

Discuss
a. Where do you usually get the weather report?
b. What is the weather going to be tomorrow? What will you wear?
c. Do you prefer cold weather or hot weather? Why?

10 Sentences with *If* Clauses

If the weather is nice tomorrow, they'll go to the beach.

Two Forms of Sentences with *If*

If + subject + verb, subject + verb
Subject + verb + *if* + subject + verb
Examples: If it rains tomorrow, we will bring an umbrella.
We will bring an umbrella if it rains tomorrow.
If my back hurts, I always lie down.
I always lie down if my back hurts.

If with Present Tense

Examples: If my son doesn't understand his homework, I help him.
We usually win if we play well.

If with Imperative

Examples: If you watch TV, turn down the volume.
Please don't tell him if he asks you.

If with Modal and Verb

Modals include *can, might, should,* and *must.*

Examples: If you are hungry, I can make a sandwich for you.

You must check in at the office if you are late.

If the baby wakes up, she might want a bottle.

If with Future Tense

Examples: If we have money next year, we will buy a new car.

I'll tell the teacher if you are sick tomorrow.

Exercise 1

Circle the verbs. Identify each verb as present, imperative, modal, or future.

1. If the store (is) closed, we (will come back) tomorrow.

   Types of verbs: __present; future__

2. If our team wins, everyone will be happy.

   Types of verbs: _____

3. You shouldn't drink a lot of soda if you want good teeth.

   Types of verbs: _____

4. If you don't like your job, look for a different job.

   Types of verbs: _____

5. A police officer might give you a ticket if you drive too fast.

   Types of verbs: _____

6. If there is a sale at the mall, call me.

   Types of verbs: _____

7. If we get a dog, who is going to take care of it?

   Types of verbs: _____

8. I watch videos if I have free time.

   Types of verbs: _____

Exercise 2: Dictation

Write the sentences that the teacher reads.

1. _____

2. _____

3. _____

4. _____

Exercise 3

Fix any mistakes.

1. If is cold in the morning Jeremy get out of bed very slow.

2. Mrs. Lane she does not feeling very well. If I'll have time tomorrow, I might visit him.

3. If we go on a picnic this weekend, I'll bring the food, and you can bring the drinks.

4. My friends will stay in this city if they can finding good jobs here.

5. Maria will very happy, if she get her driver's license soon.

6. If I am not pay my rent on time next month, the manager get very angry.

Discuss

a. Do you usually get out of bed fast?
b What foods do you bring on a picnic?
c. Are you going to stay in this city? Why or why not?
d. At what age can people get a driver's license in your home country?
e. Do you pay rent? If yes, when? If no, why?

Exercise 4

Circle the correct words.

1. (Is It is) hot today. If it (is will be might be) hot again tomorrow, we (go going will go) (in to at) the beach.

2. My first class is (in at) 7:30 a.m., and it (difficult is difficult) for me to get up early. My teacher (is does will be) (anger angry) if I (am comes will be) late for class again.

3. That boxer (work out works out is work out) every day (from for) eight hours. If he (win wins will win) his next match, he (get will get have) a lot of money.

4. You should (buy to buy) your airplane ticket now. You (pays are paying will pay) more if you (wait will wait waiting) until (next the next) month.

Discuss

a. If the weather is hot, where do you go and what do you do?
b. Do you like early classes? If yes, why? If no, why?
c. Do you like boxing? Why or why not?
d. Do you have an airplane ticket now? If yes, where are you going?

Exercise 5

Fill in the blanks. Add any necessary words.

1. If she _____ her GED, she _____ a job training
              (get)   (enter)
   program next fall.

2. My car battery _____ almost dead. If my car _____
                          (be)   (not start)
   tomorrow, _____ me a ride?
                          (you can give)

3. Next month, Tom _____ a new computer if _____
                         (buy)   (have)
   enough money.

4. If you _____ the bus, you _____ for work.
               (miss)   (late)

Exercise 6

Write sentences. Keep the order of the words.

1. if / cold tomorrow / we / wear our coats

   <u>If it is cold tomorrow, we will wear our coats.</u>

2. if / there / be / emergency / call 911

   _____

3. if / there be / good program / TV tonight / we / watch it

   _____

4. I / be / grumpy / if / I / not get / enough sleep

   _____

5. if / rain / tomorrow / we / won't go camping

   _____

6. tell me / if / she / change / mind

   _____

7. if you / not wear / seat belt / you / get seriously hurt

   _____

Discuss

a. Is there an emergency telephone number in your home country? What is it?

b. Are you going to watch TV tonight? If yes, what will you watch?

c. Are you often grumpy? How much sleep do you usually get?

d. Do you like camping? Why or why not?

e. What does it mean to "change your mind"?

Exercise 7

Complete the questions and write answers. Discuss with a partner.

1. What _____ (you will do) if there _____ (be) a war in your home country?

   If _____.

2. If a person _____ (drive) too fast, what might _____ (happen)?

   If _____.

3. What should a person _____ (do) if he _____ (lose) his passport?

   If _____.

4. If you _____ (have) enough time and money this weekend, what

   _____ (you / do)?

   If _____.

Exercise 8

Complete the sentences. Use your own ideas.

1. If I need help _____.

2. Class might be canceled if _____.

3. If my friend is sick _____.

4. I will be happy if _____.

5. I will not be happy if _____.

6. If I have time _____.

7. If my dream comes true _____.

11 Forms of *Other*

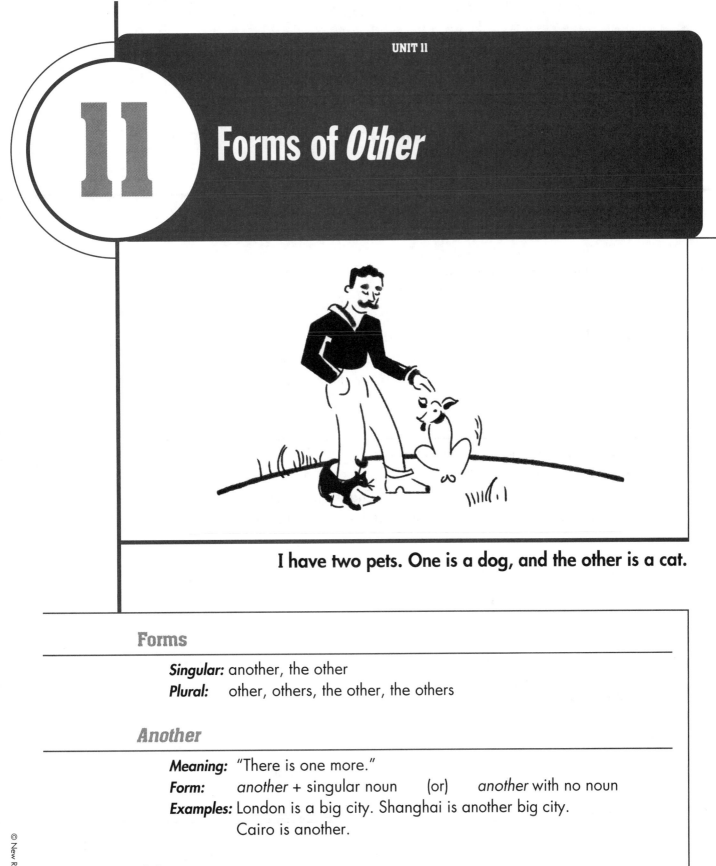

I have two pets. One is a dog, and the other is a cat.

Forms

Singular: another, the other
Plural: other, others, the other, the others

Another

Meaning: "There is one more."
Form: *another* + singular noun   (or)   *another* with no noun
Examples: London is a big city. Shanghai is another big city.
              Cairo is another.

Other

Meaning: "There are more."
Form: *other* + plural noun
Examples: Basketball is a popular sport. Tennis and golf are other sports.
              Apples and oranges are fruits. Other fruits are grapes and bananas.

Others

Meaning: "There are more."
Form: *others* + no noun
Examples: Basketball is a popular sport. Tennis and golf are others.
Apples and oranges are fruits. Others are grapes and bananas.

The other

Meaning: "There are no more besides this/these."
Form: *the other* + singular noun
(or)
the other with no noun
(or)
the other + plural noun
Examples: I have two cars. One car is old, and the other car is new.
I have two cars. One is old, and the other is new.
Six students are men, and the other students are women.

The others

Meaning: "There are no more besides these."
Form: *the others* + no noun
Example: There are twenty-six letters in the English alphabet. Twenty-one
of the letters are consonants, and the others are vowels.

Exercise 1: Dictation

Write the sentences that the teacher reads.

1. _____ Central America.

   Honduras _____ Guatemala _____ .

2. Tuna _____ .

   _____ salmon _____ halibut.

3. California _____ coast.

   _____ Los Angeles, _____ San Diego

   and San Francisco.

4. _____ Japanese flag _____ .

   _____ .

Exercise 2

Complete the sentences with words or phrases from the list. You may use a word or phrase more than once.

other	another	the others
the other one	others	the other

1. Tokyo is a very busy city, and Mexico City is _____.
   _____ busy cities are Sao Paolo and Shanghai.

2. Some people drink coffee in the morning; _____ drink tea.

3. There are two major religions in Egypt. One is Islam and _____ is Christianity.

4. Mr. Martin has four children. One is a university student, _____ is in high school, and _____ are in elementary school.

5. I looked at two stereo systems, and I am going to buy this one. I like _____ better, but it is too expensive.

6. Rachel likes one radio station, while Ben prefers _____. They listen to one station for an hour; then they listen to _____ station.

Discuss

a. What are some other busy cities?
b. What do you usually drink in the morning?
c. Do you have children? If yes, how old are they?
d. What is your favorite radio station? Why do you like it?

Exercise 3

Fix any mistakes.

1. There are many country in Africa. One is Senegal; other is Kenya.

2. Some people like American cars. The others like German car.

3. Earth is a planet. Jupiter and Mars are other planets.

4. My dog has two different eyes. One eye is blue, and

   another is brown.

5. One of my cousins plays basketball. Others all play hockey.

Discuss

a. What are some other countries in Africa?

b. What are some American cars? What are some German cars?

c. Do you have a dog? If yes, what color is it?
   What color are its eyes?

d. What sports are popular in your family?

Exercise 4

Circle the correct words.

1. Maria is a (common name   name common) for (girl   girls)
   (in   at   on) Spain. Carmen is (the other   another   other).

2. Two common family (name   names) in Japan (is   are) Sato and
   Tanaka. (Other   Another) common family name (is   are) Suzuki.

3. My sister (has   have   is have) three (son   sons). One of the
   (boy   boys) (is   are) Timothy, and (others   the other   the others)
   (is   are) Douglas and Paul.

4. In some (country   countries), people (has   have   are having) two
   (name   names). In (other   others   the other) countries, people
   (has   have   are having) three.

Exercise 5

Complete the questions and answers. Discuss with a partner.

1. What _____ your two favorite colors for clothes?
   (be)

   One _____ _____, and
   (be)

   _____ _____.
   (other / be)

2. Where _____ to go during your free time?
   (you like)

   One place _____ _____, and
   (be)

   _____ _____.
   (other / be)

3. Who _____ your three favorite writers?
   (be)

   One of my three favorite writers _____ _____.
   (be)

   _____ _____, and
   (other / be)

   _____ _____.
   (other / be)

4. What foods _____ popular in your home country?
   (be)

   One popular food _____ _____, and
   (be)

   _____ _____.
   (other / be)

Exercise 6

Write sentences. Some items need two sentences. Keep the word order and punctuate correctly.

1. tomorrow / we / going / other / quiz

   _____

2. I / reading / two book / interesting / other / boring

   _____

3. February / have 28 day / other month / have / 30 or 31

   _____

4. my computer / not work / very good / so / I / buy / other

   _____

Exercise 7

Write pairs of sentences about your classmates.

1. _____
   (there / many intelligent student / class)

   _____
   (one / be / and / other / be)

2. _____
   (today / some student / wear)

   _____
   (other / wear / today)

3. _____
   (some student / have / [color] / hair)

   _____
   (other / have / [color] / hair)

4. _____
   (some of the student / drive / school)

   _____
   (other students)

Exercise 8

Write sentences about the topics.

1. some people in this country / other people

   _____

2. some teachers / others

   _____

3. one of my favorite movies / another

   _____

4. some of the students in my class / the others

   _____

5. most of my relatives live / others

   _____

12 Past Tense of the Verb *Be*

He was sick yesterday.

Past-Tense Forms of *Be*

Past	Past Negative	Contractions
I was	I was not	I wasn't
you were	you were not	you weren't
he/she/it was	he/she/it was not	he/she/it wasn't
we were	we were not	we weren't
you were	you were not	you weren't
they were	they were not	they weren't

Examples: Yesterday Jim was absent. Bob was not here either.

I wasn't late for class last week.

At 10:00 last night, we were not at home. We were at a friend's house.

Past-Tense Questions with *Be*

Was I . . . ?
Were you . . . ?
Was he/she/it . . . ?
Were we . . . ?
Were you . . . ?
Were they . . . ?
Examples: Were you in class yesterday?
         Was it very hot last summer?
         When were your parents in Paris?

Common Past Time Expressions

last night, last year, last summer
three months ago, many years ago
in 1999, in the 20th century
yesterday
when I was a child, when we were young, when I was in school
Examples: The mall was crowded last night.
         Four years ago, I was still in my home country.
         When I was a child, our house was not very big.

Exercise 1: Dictation

Write the sentences that the teacher reads.

1. _____

2. _____

3. _____

4. _____

5. _____

Discuss

a. Where were you last night at 8:00?
b. Were you angry yesterday? How were you feeling?
c. In school, what sports or activities were you good at?
d. How long are most movies?
e. What is (was) your father's job? What is (was) your mother's job?

Exercise 2

Circle words to make true sentences. Then discuss with a partner.

1. Last night, (was it is it was) (cold not cold).

2. When I (am was were) a child, my room (are was were)
   usually (neat messy).

3. When I (was were) in first grade, my (teacher teachers)
   (was were was not were not) nice.

4. The last quiz (is was is not was not) (difficult difficultly).

5. Usually, my grades now (was is were are)
   (good so-so not good).

6. (Before many years Many years ago), life in my country
   (is was are were) (the same as now better worse).

Exercise 3

Fix any mistakes.

1. On 1776, George III is King of England.

2. The game last weekend boring.

3. The last summer, it very hot.

4. We were asleep at 11:30 last night.

5. Columbus no was the first person in America.

6. Ago 30 years, computers very expensive.

7. The first computers are more big than computers today.

Discuss

a. Was there ever a king in your home country?
   Who is the leader now?
b. How was the weather yesterday? How is the weather today?
c. Who were the first people in your home country?

Exercise 4

Complete the sentences. Use the names of people you know.
Add necessary words.

1. _____ _____ late for class last week.
                              (be)

2. _____ and _____

   _____ last week.
                              (not sick)

3. Yesterday, _____ and _____

   _____ very busy.
        (be)

4. Last night at 9:00, _____ _____ at the library.
                                                    (be not)

5. _____ _____ here right now.
                              (not)

6. Last week, _____ _____ on vacation.
                                        (not)

7. _____ and _____ _____ best
                                                    (be)

   friends many years ago.

Exercise 5

Fill in the blanks. Use the affirmative or the negative to make true
sentences. Add necessary words.

1. My parents _____ co-workers many years ago.
                      (be)

2. The first airplanes _____ than today's jets.
                              (be / small)

3. Last week, we _____ very busy.
                        (be)

4. Fifty years ago, my hometown _____.
                                              (very big)

5. _____ in Florida.
              (usually cold)

6. Yesterday, I _____ tired.
                      (be)

7. In the early 1900s, India _____ independent country.
                                        (be)

   _____ British colony.
              (be)

Exercise 6

Complete the questions and write answers. Discuss with a partner.

1. Where _____ 6:00 p.m. yesterday evening?
   (you / be)

   _____

   _____

2. Who _____ the first leader of your country?
   (be)

   _____

   _____

3. What color _____ your first car (or) your first bike?
   (be)

   _____

   _____

4. How _____ the weather yesterday?
   (be)

   _____

   _____

5. Where _____ born?
   (you / be)

   _____

   _____

6. What _____ your favorite classes in school?
   (be)

   _____

   _____

7. How old _____ in the year 2000?
   (your home country / be)

   _____

   _____

8. Who _____ your friends when you _____ a child?
   (be)   (be)

   _____

   _____

Exercise 7

Write the dialogue.

1. _____
   (how / your dinner / restaurant last night?)

   _____
   (it / great!)

2. _____
   (really? / how / food?)

   _____
   (the soup and vegetables / really delicious!)

3. _____
   (your meal / expensive?)

   _____
   (no / not expensive)

4. _____
   (how / the service?)

   _____
   (it / excellent / the waiters / very polite)

5. _____
   (you / going / eat there again?)

   _____
   (you bet! I / going / there again next week!)

Exercise 8

Write this version of the dialogue.

1. _____
   (how / your dinner / restaurant last night?)

   _____
   (it / terrible!)

2. _____
   (really? / how / food?)

   _____
   (vegetables / cold / and / meat / tough!)

3. _____
   (your meal / expensive?)

   _____
   (well / not cheap)

4. _____
   (how / the waiters?)

   _____
   (they / slow / and / impolite)

5. _____
   (you / going / eat there again?)

   _____
   (no way! never going / eat there again)

Exercise 9

Complete the sentences. Then share with a partner.

1. When I was a child, my favorite foods _____.
   (be)

2. When I was a child, I _____.
   (be afraid of)

3. When I was a child, my favorite toy _____.
   (be)

4. When I was a child, my favorite games _____.
   (be)

5. When I was a child, my favorite holiday _____.
   (be)

6. When I was a child, my life _____.
   (be)

Exercise 10

Complete the sentences.

1. Twenty-five years ago, my parents _____.
   (be)

2. Last winter, the weather _____.
   (be not)

3. Last week, my classes _____.
   (be)

4. Last night at 10:00, I _____.
   (be)

5. In school, my grades _____.
   (be not)

6. One hundred years ago, my country _____.
   (be)

There Was and There Were

Last night, there was a big fire in my neighborhood.

Meaning

There was = past tense of "there is"
There were = past tense of "there are"
Examples: There are some visitors in our class today.
Yesterday there were some visitors in our class.

Form

There was + singular subject
There were + plural subject
Examples: Last night, there was a party at my neighbor's house.
Many years ago, there were dinosaurs on Earth.

Questions

Was there . . . ?
Were there . . . ?
Examples: Was there an accident near your house last night?
         Why were there police cars on your street last night?

Negatives

There was/were + not/no/not any . . .
Examples: When I was a child, there was not a factory in my city.
         When I was a child, there was no factory in my city.
         When I was a child, there were no factories in my region.

         There wasn't any news about my country in yesterday's paper.
         There was no news about my country in yesterday's newspaper.

         There weren't any good programs on TV last night.
         There were no good programs on TV last night.

Exercise 1: Dictation

Write the sentences that the teacher reads.

1. _____

2. _____

3. _____

4. _____

5. _____

Discuss

a. Was there any rain in your city last week?
    How often do you have rain?
b. Was there a party last weekend? What did you do last weekend?
c. Is there a park near your home? Where is the closest park?
d. Do you spend a lot of time on the phone? Who do you often call?
e. Were there any students from other countries in your school?

Exercise 2

Circle the correct words.

1. In the 1900s, (it   there) (is   are   was   were) many (war   wars).
   A lot of (country   countries) (change   changed) (they   their) names.

2. (It   There) (are   was   were) one easy question (in   on) (we   us   our)
   last test. The (other   others) questions (are   was   were) difficult.

3. (Is   Were) there life on (other   others) planets? Some people
   (say   says) yes. (Other   Others) people (no believe   do not believe)
   this.

4. When I (am   was) a child, I (am   was   were) scared of many
   (thing   things). For example, (in the   at) night I (afraid   was afraid)
   that there (are   was   were) monsters in my room.

5. (Last   The last) night, the sky (is   was   were) very clear. There
   (was   were) no moon, but there (was   were) millions of (star   stars).

6. Yesterday, our teacher (sick   is sick   was sick), (but   so) there
   (weren't   wasn't) (no   any) class.

Discuss

a. Is there life on other planets? What do you think?
b. When you were a child, what were you afraid of?

Exercise 3

Fix any mistakes.

1. Yesterday, there is a big football game at the stadium.

2. There was cold the last night.

3. In newspaper yesterday, there were no article about my country.

4. In August 17, 1999, it was a big earthquake in Turkey.

5. Last Friday afternoon, there were an important meeting at school.

6. There was a lot of cockroach in my last apartment.

Exercise 4

Fill in the blanks.

1. Originally, there _____ only 13 states in the United States.
   (be)

   There _____ 50 states today.
   (be)

2. Three hundred _____ ago, there _____ a king in
   (year)   (be)

   France. Now, France _____ a king.
   (not have)

3. In the 1800s, there _____no subways in London, but today London's
   (be)

   subways _____.
   (famous)

4. After World War II, there _____ two countries in Germany: West
   (be)

   Germany and East Germany. Today, there _____ one Germany.
   (be)

5. There _____ 15 republics in the former Soviet Union.
   (be)

   The _____ republic was Russia. Now, the former republics
   (big)

   _____ independent _____.
   (be)   (country)

Discuss

a. What were some of the original American states?

b. Does your home country have a king or a president
   or a prime minister?

c. Are there any subways in your city?

d. When was World War II? How was your home country
   affected by the war?

e. What are some of the countries that were formerly
   Soviet republics?

f. Do you know anyone from Russia?

Exercise 5

Write questions and answers. Use *there was* or *there were*.

1. Question: <u>Was there a</u> _____ holiday last week?

   Answer: <u>No, there wasn't a holiday.</u> _____

2. Question: _____ any sales at the mall last weekend?

   Answer: _____

3. Question: _____ election in your home country last year?

   Answer: _____

4. Question: _____ any sports games on TV last night?

   Answer: _____

5. Question: _____ full moon last night?

   Answer: _____

Exercise 6

Write sentences. Use the verb *be*.

1. last night / there / two / interest / program / TV

   _____

2. yesterday / there / accident / front / my house

   _____

3. there / big fire / my neighborhood / last weekend

   _____

4. there / lot / mosquito / my room / last night

   _____

5. last Monday / I / late / because / there / lot / traffic

   _____

Exercise 7

Write sentences. Express your own ideas.

1. A long time ago in my neighborhood, there / a lot of

   _____

   _____

2. When I / a child, there / not many

   _____

   _____

3. Last year in my home country, there / a

   _____

   _____

4. One hundred years ago in my hometown, there / no

   _____

   _____

5. Thousands of years ago, there / not any

   _____

   _____

6. Last week, there

   _____

   _____

Past Tense of Regular Verbs

Last Saturday, we listened to some music and danced.

Form: verb + -ed

Present	Past
play	played
wash	washed

Example: Last night, he played the piano.

Questions: *did* + subject + verb

Examples: Did you wash your car yesterday? Yes, I did. (or) No, I didn't.
Why did you move? I moved because my old apartment was noisy.

Negative: *did not* + verb

Examples: Last week, it did not rain.
When I was a child, I did not study English.

Spelling

Present	Past
dream	dreamed
study	studied
cry	cried
close	closed
drop	dropped
happen	happened
occur	occurred

Exercise 1: Dictation

Write the words that the teacher reads. Then write the past affirmative and past negative.

	Present	Past Affirmative	Past Negative
1.	*pull*	*pulled*	*did not pull*
2.			
3.			
4.			
5.			
6.			
7.			
8.			

Exercise 2

Fill in the blanks to make true statements. Then discuss with a partner.

1. Last weekend, it _____.
   (rain / not rain)

2. I _____ breakfast every day.
   (have / not have)

3. I _____ English in elementary school.
   (study / not study)

4. Yesterday, I _____ video games.
   (play / not play)

5. Last night, I _____ a computer.
   (use / not use)

Exercise 3

Circle the correct words.

1. (Before many years   Many years ago), every (student   students) in Europe (study   was study   studied) Latin. Now, not many (student   students) (learn   learns   learned) Latin.

2. George Washington (is   was) the first president of (United States   the United States), but he (no lived   did not live   did not lived) in Washington, D.C. As president, Washington (lives   lived) (in   at   on) New York, the first U.S. capital, and then in Philadelphia, the second capital. Today, the U.S. president (live   lives   lived) in the White House in Washington, D.C.

3. Washington (no died   did not die   did not died) in office. He (retire   retired) and (die   died   was died) at home in Virginia.

4. Pelé (not played   did not play   did not played) American football. He (was   were) from Brazil, and he (play   was played   played) soccer. Many (people   peoples) think Pelé (was   were) (the great   the greatest   the most great) soccer player in history.

5. Long ago, Muslim scientists (develop   were developed   developed) algebra. (Today   In today), students around the world (study   studies   studied) algebra.

6. Engineers (start   started   was start) the Panama Canal (in   at   on) 1904. The work (is   was   did) very difficult, and the engineers (not finish   not finished   did not finish) until 1914.

Discuss

a. What languages did you study? When?

b. Who was the first leader of your home country?

c. Where does the leader of your home country live?

d. Did anyone famous die last year? Who died?

e. What countries have good soccer teams? Do you have a favorite team?

f. Did you study algebra? If yes, when? Was it easy or difficult?

g. Where is the Panama Canal? What oceans does it connect?

Exercise 4

Complete the questions and write answers.

1. Who _____ yesterday?
   (you / talk to)

   _____

2. What time _____ today?
   (the class start)

   _____

3. Last night, how long _____ TV?
   (you / watch)

   _____

4. Who in your class usually _____ to school?
   (walk)

   _____

5. How many questions _____ in the last class?
   (you / answer)

   _____

Exercise 5

Fix any mistakes.

1. We arrive here 3 year ago.

2. The last night, you did not turned off the computer.

3. They did not read newspaper yesterday.

4. I not feel very well last Saturday, so I was stay in bed all day.

5. She cooks a delicious dinner for we last night.

6. Miguel immigrated to Canada in 1998.

Discuss

a. When did you arrive in this city?
b. Did you read the newspaper yesterday? How often do you read it?
c. When was the last time you were sick? Did you stay in bed all day?
d. Did you cook dinner last night? What did you eat?

Write sentences.

1. rain / yesterday / but / right now / not rain

   _____

2. last Sunday / we / try / new restaurant / enjoy / meal

   _____

3. my best friend / move / another city / last year

   _____

4. some employees / work / double shift / last Saturday

   _____

5. something terrible / happen / a few days ago

   _____

6. less than a week ago, / my neighbor house / burn down

   _____

7. right now / they / live / apartment

   _____

8. last night, I / close / windows / and / turn on / heater

   _____

9. she / recently change / that tire / because / flat

   _____

Discuss

a. When did you move here?

b. Do you have friends in other cities or countries? Where?

c. What happened in your neighborhood recently?

d. Did your car ever have a flat tire? If yes, what did you do?

Exercise 7

Complete the sentences. Use the verb and give information about the
topic in parentheses. Then discuss with a partner.

1. When I was a child, my family _____ in _____.
   (live)   (city)

2. I _____ _____ a lot when I was a child.
   (play)   (sport or game)

3. I often _____ _____ when I was a child.
   (watch)   (program or activity)

4. When I was a child, my father _____ _____.
   (work)   (place)

5. I _____ _____ when I was a child.
   (not like)   (food)

6. When I was a child, my family often _____ _____.
   (visit)   (person)

7. When I was a child, I _____ if I _____.
   (cry)   (be)

Exercise 8

Write sentences with the words. Use the past tense and time
expressions (e.g., *yesterday, last night, two weeks ago*).

1. play

   My brother played soccer last weekend.

2. wait for

   _____

3. help

   _____

4. not enjoy

   _____

5. use

   _____

UNIT 15

Past Tense of Irregular Verbs 1

15

Yesterday, he ate a hot dog for lunch.

Some Irregular Verbs

Present	Past	Past Negative
buy	bought	did not buy
come	came	did not come
do	did	did not do
eat	ate	did not eat
feel	felt	did not feel
find	found	did not find
go	went	did not go
have	had	did not have
know	knew	did not know
make	made	did not make
read	read (/red/)	did not read
run	ran	did not run
say	said (/sed/)	did not say
see	saw	did not see

More Irregular Verbs

Present	Past	Past Negative
steal	stole	did not steal
take	took	did not take
tell	told	did not tell
write	wrote	did not write

Examples: She wrote a letter yesterday.

Last Friday, we went to a party.

Questions

Form: *did* + subject + simple form of verb

Examples: Did you eat breakfast?

What did he say?

Negatives

Form: *did not/didn't* + simple form of the verb

Examples: I did not have time.

He didn't say anything.

Other Irregular Verbs

For a list of irregular verbs, see Appendix 1.

Exercise 1: Dictation

Write the sentences that the teacher reads. Then discuss. Are any sentences true for your class?

1. _____

2. _____

3. _____

4. _____

5. _____

6. _____

7. _____

Exercise 2

Circle the correct words.

1. Yesterday, we (go   were go   went) to (a   an) fancy restaurant. We (have   has   had) steak, and it (did   was   is) delicious.

2. I usually (write   wrote) to my parents (in   on) weekends, but last week I (not had   did not have   do not have) time.

3. When I was a teenager, I (eat   ate   eating) a lot of junk food, but now I (buy   bought) food that (is   were) (good   well) for my health.

4. Edward (enjoy   enjoys) languages. (Last year   The last year) he (takes   took   taked) a German class.
   Right now he (studied   study   is studying) Spanish.

5. (Last   At last) night, Amy (go   was go   went) (to   at) bed (to   at) 3:30 a.m. because she (read   readed   reads) a book until 3:00.

Discuss

a. Where did you have dinner last night?

b. What kinds of junk food do you eat? Did you eat any recently?

c. What did you read last night? What time did you go to bed?

Exercise 3

Fix any mistakes.

1. yesterday I did not saw my neighbors.

2. On 1990, his family buy a new house.

3. When he was a child, Jeffrey never eat carrots.

4. it did not be very hot last week.

5. When I saw Mrs. Chang, she say she had a headache.

6. Before class, teacher told us her office telephone number.

Exercise 4

Complete the sentences. Use verbs from the list.

ask	do	go	read
be	eat	know	run
buy	find	not have	write

1. We _____ pizza for dinner last night. It _____

   delicious.

2. Last weekend, I _____ to a party at my friend's house.

3. I was late for class, so I _____ to school.

4. The teacher _____ me a question yesterday, and I

   _____ the answer.

5. Last Saturday, my mother _____ me an e-mail message.

6. When I was a child, I _____ $10 on the street.

7. I _____ an interesting article in yesterday's newspaper.

8. Last night, I _____ my homework at the library.

9. Last year, my friend _____ a used car because he

   _____ enough money for a new one.

Discuss

a. What did you have for dinner last night?

b. Where did you go last weekend?

c. Did the teacher ask you any questions today?
   Did you know the answers?

d. Did you read the newspaper yesterday?
   What newspaper do you read?

e. When did you buy your first car? What kind of car was it?

Exercise 5

Complete the questions and write answers. Discuss with a partner.

1. What _____ for breakfast this morning?
   (you / have)

   _____

2. When you _____ young, who _____ letters to?
   (be)   (you / write)

   _____

3. What _____ at the beginning of class today?
   (the teacher / say)

   _____

4. What time _____ bed last night?
   (you / go)

   _____

5. What _____ last week?
   (you / buy)

   _____

Exercise 6

Write sentences.

1. last month / I / have / a lot / of meetings

   _____

2. I / feel / sick / yesterday, so I / go / home / early

   _____

3. we / take / test / last week, and everyone / do / well

   _____

4. some / my friends / see / that movie / week ago

   _____

5. when my sister and I / be / child, / read / lot of book

   _____

Exercise 7

Fill in the blanks.

1. It _____ the Egyptians many years to build the pyramids.
   (take)

2. The Chinese _____ the first eyeglasses.
   (make)

   Today, millions of people _____ glasses.
   (wear)

3. Many years ago, people _____ to North America from Asia.
   (come)

   There _____ a land bridge between Asia and America.
   (be)

4. In the 15th century, some scientists _____ that
   (know)

   Earth _____ around the Sun, but most people
   (go)

   _____ them.
   (not believe)

5. Shakespeare _____ *Romeo and Juliet* in the 16th century.
   (write)

   Many students _____ it in school these days.
   (read)

6. In 1867, the United States _____ Alaska from Russia.
   (buy)

   It _____ much—only about $7 million.
   (not cost)

7. In the 1950s, scientists _____ some very old human bones in Africa.
   (find)

   The bones _____ more than 1 million years old.
   (be)

8. Many Native Americans today _____ that the first Europeans in
   (say)

   America _____ their land.
   (steal)

Discuss

a. What is a famous place in your home country?
b. Who were the first people in your home country?
c. Do you wear glasses? When do you wear them?
d. Did you ever read anything by Shakespeare? If yes, what was it?
e. Is anyone in your family a scientist? Do you like science?
f. Did you ever study history? What time in history interests you most?

Exercise 8

Write sentences with the words. Use the past tense and time expressions (e.g., *yesterday, last night, two weeks ago*).

1. eat

   I ate sushi for dinner last night.

2. come

   _____

3. not see

   _____

4. find

   _____

5. are

   _____

6. not go

   _____

7. tell

   _____

8. take

   _____

9. feel

   _____

10. not run

   _____

11. buy

   _____

16 Past Tense of Irregular Verbs 2

Last year, she gave her father a watch for his birthday.

Some Irregular Verbs

Present	Past	Past Negative
break	broke	did not break
drink	drank	did not drink
fall	fell	did not fall
get	got	did not get
give	gave	did not give
grow	grew	did not grow
hear	heard	did not hear
leave	left	did not leave
meet	met	did not meet
pay	paid	did not pay
ride	rode	did not ride

More Irregular Verbs

Present	Past	Past Negative
speak	spoke	did not speak
think	thought	did not think
understand	understood	did not understand
wake	woke	did not wake

Examples: He spoke to his sister last night.

I did not understand the movie very well.

Did you understand the speaker at the conference last night?

Who did you speak to about the problem yesterday?

We didn't speak to each other yesterday.

Past Tense of *Can: Could*

Present	Past	Past Negative
can	could	could not/couldn't

Examples: Could you answer all of the questions on the test yesterday?

They couldn't find our house.

Why couldn't you come to the party last weekend?

Other Irregular Verbs

For a list of irregular verbs, see Appendix 1.

Exercise 1: Dictation

Write the sentences that the teacher reads.

1. _____

2. _____

3. _____

4. _____

5. _____

Discuss

a. Did you understand the grammar in the last class?

b. Do you have a bike? If yes, when did you last ride your bike?

c. Do you have a camera? If yes, when did you last take pictures?

d. Who is your best friend? When did you meet him or her?

Exercise 2

Fix any mistakes.

1. In high school, I cannot spoke English.

2. He absent the last Monday because he not feel very well.

3. We did not leave school yesterday until 9:00 p.m.

4. My parent get married many year ago.

5. When we was children, we drank a lot milk.

6. When I was young, I think a man lived in the Moon.

Discuss

a. Did you study English in school? Could you speak it?
b. What time did you leave school yesterday?
c. Did you drink a lot of milk when you were a child? What about now?

Exercise 3

Complete the questions and write answers. Discuss with a partner.

1. When _____ your best friend for the first time?
   (you / meet)

   _____

2. What _____ your father for his birthday?
   (you / give)

   _____

3. What _____ when you _____ child?
   (you / cannot / do)   (be)

   _____

4. Who _____ on the phone yesterday?
   (you / speak to)

   _____

5. In school, what subject _____ very well?
   (you / not understand)

   _____

Exercise 4

Circle the correct words.

1. A long time ago, people (think   thought   were think) the Earth (flat   was flat). Now, most people (know   knew   knows) the Earth (is round   round   was round).

2. Last week, Mr. Ray (had   made   did) (a   an) accident. He (fall   fell   falled) down the stairs and (breaked   broked   broke) his arm.

3. Yesterday, (we   our   us) friend (tell   told) (we   us) some sad news. (We   Us) (cryed   cried) when (we   us) (heared   heard   hears) it.

4. (Last night   The last night), Mari (get   getted   got) very sick. (Morning   This morning), she still (felt   feel   feeled) ill, so she (couldn't go   can't went) to work.

Discuss

a. Did you ever break your arm or another bone? What happened?
b. Did you get any sad news recently? What happened?
c. How did you feel yesterday?

Exercise 5

Write sentences. Fill the blanks with names of people you know.

1. In school, / _____ / ride / bike / every day

   _____

2. _____ / not speak / English / home / when / child

   _____

3. In school, / _____ / get / good grades / math

   _____

4. The other day, / _____ / leave / homework / home

   _____

Exercise 6

Write sentences. Use the past tense.

1. last weekend, / my family / go / the mountains

   _____

2. we / leave / Friday afternoon

   _____

3. we / get back / Sunday night

   _____

4. it / cold / the morning, so / we / drink / hot chocolate

   _____

5. my son / fall / and / break / flashlight

   _____

6. midnight, I / wake up / and / hear / owl

   _____

7. we / not see / any other people

   _____

8. sky / very dark / and / we / can / see / lot / star

   _____

9. we / make / fire / and / tell / stories around the fire

   _____

10. it / fun / so / we / decide / to go again / next month

   _____

Discuss
a. Do you like camping? Why or why not?
b. What happened on your last vacation or adventure?

Exercise 7

Complete the sentences. Use the affirmative or negative to make true statements. Then discuss with a partner.

1. Many years ago, cowboys _____ horses.
   (ride)

   They _____ cows.
   (ride)

2. I _____ $75 for this book.
   (pay)

   I _____ .
   (pay)

3. We _____ our teacher this year.
   (meet)

   We _____ last year.
   (meet)

4. I _____ a new car for my last birthday.
   (get)

   I _____ .
   (get)

Exercise 8

Write sentences with the words. Use the past tense and time expressions (e.g., *yesterday, two weeks ago, in 1999*).

1. hear

   Last night on the radio, I heard about an accident.

2. drink

   _____

3. give

   _____

4. break

   _____

5. not understand

   _____

6. meet

   _____

17 Past Tense of Irregular Verbs 3

She sold her house last week.

Some Irregular Verbs

Present	Past	Past Negative
begin	began	did not begin
bring	brought	did not bring
build	built	did not build
catch	caught	did not catch
choose	chose	did not choose
drive	drove	did not drive
fight	fought	did not fight
fly	flew	did not fly
forget	forgot	did not forget
hold	held	did not hold
keep	kept	did not keep
lose	lost	did not lose
ring	rang	did not ring
sell	sold	did not sell

More Irregular Verbs

Present	Past	Negative Past
send	sent	did not send
shoot	shot	did not shoot
sing	sang	did not sing
sit	sat	did not sit
sleep	slept	did not sleep
spend	spent	did not spend
stand	stood	did not stand
swim	swam	did not swim
teach	taught	did not teach
throw	threw	did not throw
wear	wore	did not wear
win	won	did not win

Examples: Did you sleep well last night? Yes, I slept well.

What time did the meeting begin yesterday? It began at 3 p.m.

Verbs That Don't Change

cost	hit	let	quit	shut
cut	hurt	put	set	

Examples: He put the trash outside last night.

I did not hit the ball very well in yesterday's game.

Did you shut the door?

Other Irregular Verbs

For a list of irregular verbs, see Appendix 1.

Exercise 1: Dictation

Write the sentences that the teacher reads.

1. _____

2. _____

3. _____

4. _____

5. _____

6. _____

Exercise 2

Circle the correct words.

1. George (begin   was begin   began) smoking a long time ago, but last year, he (was quit   quitted   quit).

2. On her last birthday, Debbie's parents (said   say   was say), "You can (have   to have) either a CD player or a digital camera." Debbie (choose   chose   chosed) a CD player because (he   she) (love   loves   is love) music.

3. My sister (no have   don't have   doesn't have) a digital camera. On her last vacation, she (shoot   shooted   shot) 20 rolls of film.

4. Last night, I (shut   was shut   shutted) the windows because (it was   there was   there were) noisy outside and I (can't study   couldn't study   couldn't studied).

5. During the movie, the children (scare   scared   were scared) and (hold   held   holded) their (father   fathers   father's) hands.

6. My friends (flew   flied   fly) to Florida for a vacation last February, and I (keep   kept   keeped) their dog at my house.

7. In my last softball game, two of our players (hit   hits   hitted) home runs. We (catches   catched   caught) every ball (hit   hits   hitted) by the other team, so our team (win   winned   won   wonned).

Discuss

a. Do you know people who quit smoking? If so, who? How did they do it?

b. Do you like music? What kind do you like best?

c. Do you have a camera? If so, what kind? Do you take many photos?

d. Could you study last night? Why or why not?

e. Do you like scary movies? Why or why not?

f. Did you ever keep someone's pets while they were away? If yes, whose? What pets did they have?

g. What was the last game you played or watched? Who won? Who lost?

Exercise 3

Fix any mistakes.

1. He don't have a car now because he sold two days ago.

2. The last week, I catch a cold from one of my classmates.

3. Yesterday, the baby tired, so she sleeped all day.

4. Last month, my friends send me a package of food from my country.

5. Usually my son sets the table for dinner, but I set it last night.

6. one student's cell phone ring during class yesterday.

> ### Discuss
> a. When did you last catch a cold? How often do you get colds?
> b. How many hours did you sleep last night? Did you sleep well?
> c. What do people send you from your home country?
> d. Who usually sets the table at your house? Who set it last night?

Exercise 4

Complete the questions and write answers. Discuss with a partner.

1. Who _____ next to in class last week?
   (you / sit)

   _____

2. What kind of shoes _____ to class last week?
   (you / wear)

   _____

3. How much _____?
   (your notebook / cost)

   _____

4. What _____ to class today?
   (you bring)

   _____

5. What _____ away today?
   (you / throw)

   _____

Exercise 5

Write sentences. The sentences will form a story. Use the past tense.

1. yesterday / Brad / have / bad day

   _____

2. first, he / oversleep / because he / not set / alarm clock

   _____

3. then he / shave / but / cut / chin / because / in a hurry

   _____

4. by accident, / wear / one brown shoe / one black shoe

   _____

5. drive / work / but / lock / key / inside / car

   _____

6. then he / forget / important meeting

   _____

7. lunch, he / think / have / $25, but / can find / only $5

   _____

8. he either lose / or spend the other $20

   _____

9. final, / things / get better / Brad / afternoon

   _____

Discuss

a. Did you ever oversleep? What happened?
b. Do you usually set an alarm clock? What wakes you up?
c. Did you ever lock yourself out of your car or house?
   What did you do?
d. Did you ever lose any money? How much did you lose?

Exercise 6

Write pairs of sentences.

1. _____
   (yesterday / Mr. Ruiz / go shopping)
   _____
   (spend / lot / money)

2. _____
   (Pietro / not sleep / good / last night)
   _____
   (cannot get / comfortable)

3. _____
   (Mr. Kramer / upset / last week)
   _____
   (wife / forget / anniversary)

4. _____
   (Mr. and Mrs. Chang / have / beautiful home)
   _____
   (they / build / 1999)

5. _____
   (last year, Mia / put / lot of money / bank)
   _____
   (choose / account / careful)

6. _____
   (yesterday / teacher / stand / blackboard)
   _____
   (not sit / desk)

7. _____
   (last week / teacher / keep / we / late)
   _____
   (this week / let / we / out / early)

Discuss

a. When was the last time you went shopping? Did you spend a lot?

b. Did you sleep well last night? If not, why?

c. Are you married? If yes, when is your anniversary?

d. Did you ever build anything? If yes, what did you build?

e. Last year, did you put any money in the bank,
   or did you spend it all?

f. Does your teacher usually stand or sit during class?

g. Does your teacher usually keep you late or let you out early?

Exercise 7

Write sentences with the words. Use the past tense and time expressions such as *five years ago, yesterday, in 2001*.

1. build

   Last year, my country built many new roads.

2. wear

   _____

3. sit

   _____

4. not cost

   _____

5. sell

   _____

6. drive

   _____

7. catch

   _____

8. not lose

   _____

9. teach

   _____

10. send

   _____

11. fly

   _____

Past-Tense Questions

What time did you get up yesterday?

Questions with the Verb *Be*

Examples: Were you on time for class today? Yes, I was. (or) No, I wasn't.
Was the movie in color or black and white? It was in color.
Where were you born? I was born in Bangkok.
Why was she absent yesterday? She was absent because she was sick.

Questions with Other Verbs

Examples: Did it rain last night? Yes, it did. (or) No, it didn't.
When did you go to the doctor? I went to the doctor on Friday.
Why did you say that? I said that because I was angry.
How much did your jeans cost? They cost about $25.
What happened to your car? I had an accident.
Who called you last night? My sister called me.
Who wrote *War and Peace*? Tolstoy wrote it. (or) I don't know.

Exercise 1: Dictation

**Write the questions that the teacher reads. Then write answers.
Discuss with a partner.**

1. Question: _____

    Answer: _____

2. Question: _____

    Answer: _____

3. Question: _____

    Answer: _____

4. Question: _____

    Answer: _____

Exercise 2

Fix any mistakes. Then write answers. Discuss with a partner.

1. Question: Where did you went yesterday?

    Answer: _____

2. Question: Was enjoyable your last vacation?

    Answer: _____

3. Question: How did you feel yesterday?

    Answer: _____

4. Question: How many student are there in your last class?

    Answer: _____

5. Question: Last night, you listen music?

    Answer: _____

Exercise 3

Circle the correct words. Write answers. Then discuss with a partner.

1. Question: What (is   are   was   were) your favorite food
   when you (was   were) a child?

   Answer: _____

2. Question: (Were   Did   Do) you (have   had   having) long hair
   when you (young   are young   were young)?

   Answer: _____

3. Question: Nowadays, (are   do   did) you often (make   maked   made)
   (the dinner   dinner) at home?

   Answer: _____

4. Question: How (much   many) TV (you watch   you watched   did you watch) last night?

   Answer: _____

Exercise 4

Read the answer. Then write the question.

1. Question: _Who did Prince Charles marry?_ _____
   Answer: Prince Charles married Princess Diana.

2. Question: _____
   Answer: Neil Armstrong walked on the moon in 1969.

3. Question: _____
   Answer: No, Einstein was not a very good student in high school.

4. Question: _____
   Answer: Elvis Presley died from taking too many drugs.

5. Question: _____
   Answer: Yes, Dali and Picasso were from Spain.

Exercise 5

Write questions and answers. Then discuss with a partner.

1. you / busy / yesterday?

   Question: _____

   Answer: _____

   _____

2. what time / you / dinner / last night?

   Question: _____

   Answer: _____

   _____

3. you / breakfast / this morning?

   Question: _____

   Answer: _____

   _____

4. how / you / feel / now?

   Question: _____

   Answer: _____

   _____

5. who / you / talk to / yesterday?

   Question: _____

   Answer: _____

   _____

6. where / you / grow up?

   Question: _____

   Answer: _____

   _____

Exercise 6

Look at the pictures. Write questions and answers.

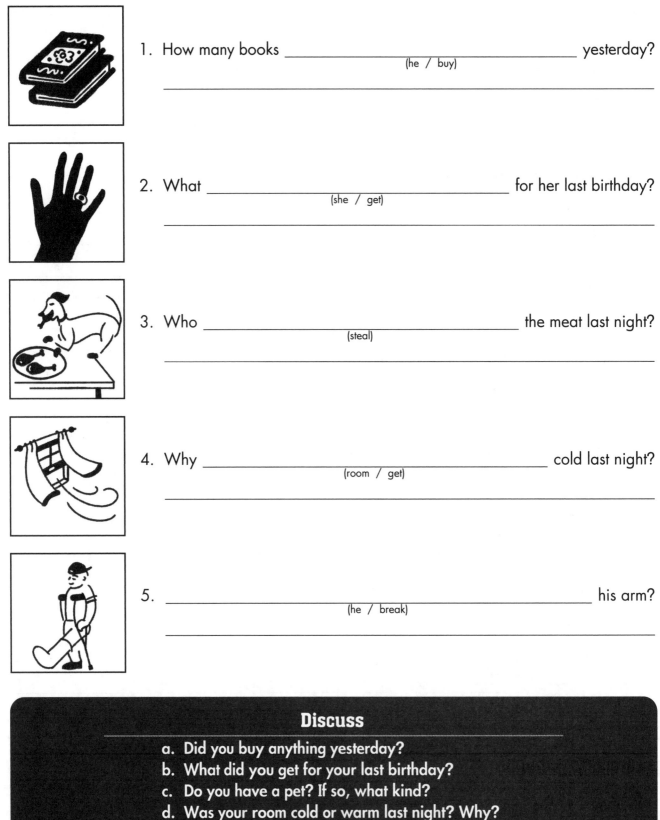

1. How many books _____ yesterday?
   (he / buy)

   _____

2. What _____ for her last birthday?
   (she / get)

   _____

3. Who _____ the meat last night?
   (steal)

   _____

4. Why _____ cold last night?
   (room / get)

   _____

5. _____ his arm?
   (he / break)

   _____

Discuss

a. Did you buy anything yesterday?

b. What did you get for your last birthday?

c. Do you have a pet? If so, what kind?

d. Was your room cold or warm last night? Why?

e. Did you ever break a bone? If yes, which bone?

Exercise 7

Complete the questions. Use the names of classmates.
Write answers. Then discuss with a partner.

1. Question: _____ late today?

   Answer: _____

2. Question: What _____ bring to class today?

   Answer: _____

3. Question: How _____ get to class today?

   Answer: _____

4. Question: _____ cell phone ring in class last week?

   Answer: _____

Exercise 8

Complete the questions and write answers. Use verbs from the box.

be	have	know	take	win

1. _____ each other when they were children?
   (your parents)

   _____

2. How many medals _____ in the last Olympic Games?
   (your home country)

   _____

3. In school, _____ a man or a woman?
   (your best teacher)

   _____

4. _____ a bus to school when you were young?
   (you)

   _____

5. What _____ for dinner last night?
   (you)

   _____

Verb + Infinitive and Verb + Gerund

She enjoys painting, and he likes to take pictures.

Forms

Infinitives	Gerunds
to go	going
to listen	listening
to speak	speaking

Verb + infinitive

Examples: They want to leave now.
He told me to call him.
She decided not to move.

Verb + noun/pronoun + infinitive

Examples: The policeman told him to get out of the car.
I need you to help me.

Verbs Often Followed by Infinitives

agree	hope	plan	tell
decide	learn	promise	try
expect	need	refuse	want
forget	offer	seem	would like

Verb + gerund

Examples: I don't enjoy washing the dishes.
He stopped smoking a long time ago.

Preposition + gerund

Examples: I am interested in meeting new people.
He always talks about changing, but he never changes.

Activity Verbs: *go* + gerund

Examples: He often goes shopping at the mall.
Can we go swimming later?
Are you going fishing?

Verbs Often Followed by Gerunds

consider	enjoy	practice	be afraid of
deny	finish	quit	be interested in
discuss	keep	stop	talk about
			think about

Verbs Followed by Either Form

Some verbs can be followed by either an infinitive or a gerund.

begin (began)	like
continue	love
hate	start

Examples: It began to rain at 6:00 last night.
(or)
It began raining at 6:00 last night.

Exercise 1: Dictation

Write the sentences that the teacher reads. Circle the verbs and
underline the infinitive or gerund.

1. _____ He plans to get another job. _____

2. _____

3. _____

4. _____

5. _____

6. _____

7. _____

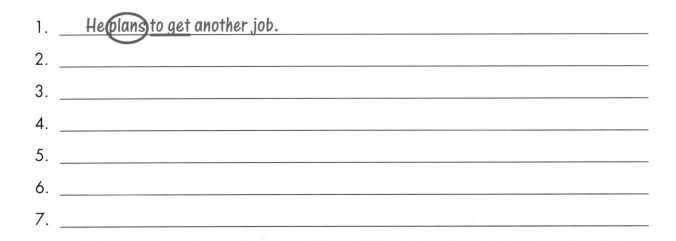

Discuss

a. Are any of these sentences true for you?

b. What are some things you are planning to do?

c. What are some things you are trying to do?

d. What are some things you enjoy? What are some things you do
not enjoy?

e. What are some things you are thinking about doing?

f. What are some things you want to do?

Exercise 2

Circle the correct words.

1. Most children (begin   begins   beginning) (walk   to walk   to walking)
   when (he   it   they) (is   are   have) 11 or 12 (month   months) old.

2. Parents (need   needs   are need) (spending   spend   to spend)
   (lot   a lot) of time with (they   them   their) children.

3. When you (is   was   were) a child, (are   were) you interested in
   (play   to play   playing) sports?

4. Some children (no like   do not like   are not like)
   (go   going   to going) (in   at   to) school.

5. Children (try often   often try) (be   to be) like (his   your   their)
   parents.

Exercise 3

Complete the sentences.

1. Adam _____ a haircut now.
   (need / get)

2. Yesterday, Megan _____ her garage.
   (begin / paint)

3. My friends and I _____.
   (love / go / camp)

4. Raymond _____ a good job
   (want / get)
   when _____.
   (finish / study)

5. Alicia _____,
   (not like / cook)
   so _____.
   (often / eat / restaurant)

6. Right now, my brother _____ a new computer.
   (consider / buy)
   His old computer just _____.
   (stop / work)

7. Most of my classmates _____
   (planning / take)
   more English classes next year.

8. My cousins _____ soon.
   (want / me / visit)

9. Some people _____.
   (afraid / fly)

10. Last year I _____ my own business.
    (think about / start)

11. Sarah _____ a roommate
    (would like / find)
    because she _____ the bills.
    (need / more money / pay)

12. Robert _____ last weekend.
    (cannot / go / hike)

Exercise 4

Complete the questions. Write answers. Discuss with a partner.

1. What _____ in your free time?

(you / enjoy / do)

   _____

2. How old _____ when you learned _____?

(you / be)   (read)

   _____

3. What _____ after class today?

(you / plan / do)

   _____

4. What are you _____ next weekend?

(think about / do)

   _____

5. What do you need _____ this week?

(buy)

   _____

6. What _____?

(you / not like / do)

   _____

Exercise 5

Fix any mistakes.

1. Mr. and Mrs. Ellis are live in Chicago right now.

2. They are thinking about move to a more small city.

3. Last night, they discussed selling their apartment.

4. They also talked about changed they jobs.

5. If they will move, they will be need to find new job.

6. they agreed to talking again tonight.

7. They hope decide in soon.

Exercise 6

Write pairs of sentences.

1. _____
   (Lucy / start / swim / when / very young)

   _____
   (now / swim / very good)

2. _____
   (Mr. Mendoza car / need / a new engine)

   _____
   (think about / get / a new car)

3. _____
   (two day ago / start / rain / morning)

   _____
   (finally stop / rain / last night)

4. _____
   (last night, I / tired, but / keep / study)

   _____
   (I / finish / work / 2 a.m.)

5. _____
   (every day he / practice / play the guitar)

   _____
   (soon / he / play / very good)

6. _____
   (last night, Tommy / refuse / eat his carrots)

   _____
   (parents / tell him / go / his room)

7. _____
   (yesterday, Ruth / not finish / do / her work)

   _____
   (today / cannot / go / movies / with us)

Discuss

a. Can you swim? If yes, when did you learn to swim?

b. Are you hoping to buy a car soon? Why or why not?

c. How often does it rain in your city?

d. Did you try to study last night? When did you finish studying?

e. Can you play a musical instrument?
   If yes, when did you learn to play?

f. When you were a child, what food did you refuse to eat?

Write sentences. Express your own ideas.

1. today the teacher / seem / be

   _____

2. these days my friend / think about / buy

   _____

3. my family / enjoy

   _____

4. my friends / often like to

   _____

5. my father / often forget to

   _____

6. my teacher / love to

   _____

7. when I was a child, my parents / tell me to

   _____

8. after I finish / study English, I

   _____

20 The Definite Article *The*

The moon is beautiful tonight.

Meaning

the = the only one
Examples: The sky is blue.
The Queen of England lives in London.

Using *The*

Introduce a word with *a* or *an,* and then use *the.*
Examples: We saw a movie last night. After the movie, we ate dinner.
He got a car last month. Now he drives the car everywhere.

With General Nouns

Do not use *the* with general nouns.
Examples: Computers are important in business.
Books tell about many topics.

With Specific Nouns

Use *the* with specific nouns.
Examples: The computer in my office is old.
The book on my desk tells about English grammar.

With Plural Nouns

When a plural noun means all of the items in a category, use *the*.
Examples: The houses in my neighborhood are not expensive.
The cherry trees in Washington, D.C., were a gift from Japan.

With Certain Nouns and Expressions

rivers and oceans:	the Yellow River, the Indian Ocean
ordinal numbers:	the first day, the second reason
with *same:*	the same price, the same country
some *of* phrases:	on the right side of the room, the history of Europe
superlatives:	the oldest building, the most wonderful story

Nouns That Don't Use *The*

people's names:	Mr. Lee, Elena
possessive nouns:	Adam's car, Mrs. Olivera's house
planets:	Jupiter, Uranus (exception: Earth or the Earth)
countries:	Russia, Mauritania (exception: the United States)
U.S. states:	Colorado, Michigan
cities:	Buenos Aires, Shanghai
languages:	English, Chinese
streets:	Highland Street, Third Street
foods:	oranges, carrots
meals:	breakfast, lunch, dinner
academic subjects:	biology, engineering
days of the week:	Friday, Wednesday
months:	October, March
some time expressions:	last week, next year, at night
sports:	soccer, volleyball

Exercise 1: Dictation

Write the sentences that the teacher reads.

1. _____

2. _____

3. _____

4. _____

5. _____

Exercise 2

Circle the correct words. Circle the dash (—) if no article is needed.

1. There is (a   the   —) very famous museum (in   at) Paris.
   (A   The   —) museum (has   have) many important
   (painting   paintings).

2. (A   The   —) Chinese is (a   the   —) difficult language.
   (Other   The other   Another) difficult language is
   (the Russian   Russian   Russia).

3. (A   The   —) Mr. Stevens (no have   not has   does not have)
   (a   the   —) car, so (walk   walks   he walks)
   (to work   the work). (Next year   The next year), he
   (is going to buy   is going to buying   going to buy)
   (a   the   —) car.

4. (An   The   —) adults (usually are   are usually)
   (more strong than   stronger than) (a   the   —) children.

5. Marta is (an   the   —) only single woman in my neighborhood. She
   (live   lives) next door to (me   my), and she is (a   the   —) doctor.

Discuss

a. What are some other famous museums, and where are they?
b. What is your first language? Is it more difficult than English?
c. Do you walk to school? If not, how do you get to school?
d. Who is usually stronger—men or women?
e. Is your doctor a man or a woman? What about your dentist?
f. Who lives next door to you? Who lives across the street?

Exercise 3

Complete the sentences. Add articles as needed.

1. From 1790 to 1800, _____ of _____
   (capital) _____ (United States)
   was _____ , _____ .
   (Philadelphia) (Pennsylvania)

2. _____ is very cold in _____ .
   (North Atlantic Ocean) (winter)

3. In general, _____ in _____ are small and
   (house) (Tokyo)
   expensive.

4. _____ in our apartment are _____ . Now, we
   (chair) (metal)
   _____ chairs made of wood.
   (think / buy)

5. _____ in _____ next to mine are noisy, but I like
   (children) (house)
   _____ in general, so I don't mind _____ .
   (children) (noise)

6. This _____ for our listening class.
   (not / book)
   _____ our grammar book.
   (be)

7. My sister reads _____ .
   (lot / magazine)
   Most of _____ are about _____ because she's
   (magazine) (science)
   _____ of _____ .
   (professor) (chemistry)

Exercise 4

Fix any mistakes.

1. Chicago is the most big city in the Illinois, but it is not capital.

2. There are a lot of water in ocean, but we cannot drink salt water.

3. I went to library at school and got book about Martin Luther King Jr.

4. I love to listen to Mia's voice. She is the best singer in the choir.

5. A refrigerator in my apartment not working right now.

Exercise 5

Complete the questions and write answers. Discuss with a partner.

1. Who _____ first leader in your country's history?
   _(be)_

   _____

   _____

2. What street _____ ?
   (you live)

   _____

   _____

3. What food _____ ?
   (vegetarians / not eat)

   _____

   _____

4. What _____ your favorite subject in school?
   _(be)_

   _____

   _____

5. _____ sky clear or cloudy today?
   _(be)_

   _____

   _____

6. _____ door of your classroom open or closed now?
   _(be)_

   _____

   _____

7. _____ water from the tap in this city?
   (you / drink)

   _____

   _____

8. Where _____ nearest zoo?
   _(is)_

   _____

   _____

Exercise 6

Write pairs of sentences.

1. _____
   (Joe / gave / wife / vacuum / diamond ring)

   _____
   (not like / vacuum, but / love / ring)

2. _____
   (we / ate / lunch / restaurant)

   _____
   (burgers / greasy / but / salad / fresh)

3. _____
   (Rosa / bought / computer / and / printer)

   _____
   (printer / cheap than / computer)

4. _____
   (Ms. Hann / works for / international company)

   _____
   (name / company / Worldwide Commerce)

Discuss

a. Where did you eat lunch yesterday? What did you have? Was it good?

b. Do you have a computer? If yes, when did you buy it?

c. Do you have a job? Where do you work?

Exercise 7

Complete the sentences. Use *a*, *an*, or *the* when needed.

1. _____, we took _____ to _____.
   (last summer)   (vacation)   (Hawaii)

   We stayed at _____ in _____.
                (hotel)   (Honolulu)

   From _____ could see _____.
        (hotel)   (ocean)

   There was _____ near _____, and
             (beautiful beach)   (hotel)

   _____ we took _____ on _____.
   (every day)   (long walks)   (beach)

2. _____, there was _____
   (yesterday)   (accident)

   in front of _____ on _____.
               (post office)   (Sixth Avenue)

   _____ hit _____.
   (car)   (bicycle rider)

   _____ fell and broke his arm.
   (rider)

Exercise 8

Write sentences with the words.

1. sun

   _____

2. president

   _____

3. store

   _____

4. Amazon River

   _____

5. busiest street

   _____

6. subject in school

   _____

7. same country

   _____

8. front of the room

   _____

9. students in my class

   _____

Connecting Words:
Before, After, When, Because

21

He washed his hands before he ate dinner.

Structures

Subject + verb *before/after/when/because* subject + verb
(or)
Before/After/When/Because subject + verb, subject + verb
(or)
before/after + noun

Examples: I always brush my teeth before I go to bed.

Before I go to bed, I always brush my teeth.

Before bed, I always brush my teeth.

I also brush my teeth after lunch.

Carolina had a baby two years after she got married.

Two years after Carolina got married, she had a baby.

People often listen to the radio when they drive.

When people drive, they often listen to the radio.

There are not many trees here because there is not much water.

Because there is not much water here, there are not many trees.

Exercise 1: Dictation

Write the sentences that the teacher reads.

1. _____

2. _____

3. _____

4. _____

Discuss

a. Do you or does anyone in your family wear glasses? Why?

Exercise 2

Circle the correct words.

1. I usually (take   am take   am taking) a shower
   (before   when   after   because) (go   I go   I am go)
   (in bed   to bed   to the bed).

2. (When   After) (take a shower   a shower),
   I (feel always   always feel) good.

3. Because I (no have   have not   do not have) time, I sometimes
   (no take   not take   don't take) a shower (in morning   in the morning).

4. Some (man   men) shave before (take   they take) a shower.
   (Other   Others   Another) (man   men) shave after (they   them) shower.

5. When (is cold   it is cold), I (like   am like   am liking)
   (take   to take   to taking) (hot   a hot) shower. But (in   at   on)
   the summer, I (enjoying   am enjoy   enjoy) (take   to take   taking)
   (cool   a cool) shower.

Discuss

a. What is your routine? What do you usually
   do before and after class?

Exercise 3

Fix any mistakes.

1. Before a person drive car, he or she must to get driver's license.

2. Ed went to the doctor last week because he felt a pain in his chest.

3. Two year ago, when she is 12 years old, Jenna begin play the piano.

4. After the game yesterday, we have dinner at a Italian restaurant.

Discuss

a. Do you have computer? If yes, why did you get it?
b. Do you have a driver's license? If yes, when did you get it?
c. What does a pain in the chest sometimes mean?
d. Who do you know who plays a musical instrument? When did they start?
e. Do you often eat in restaurants? Why? When do you go out for dinner?

Exercise 4

Complete the questions and answers. Use correct punctuation. Then discuss with a partner.

1. What (do did will) you do before you (come came) to class today?

   Before _____

2. What (do did will) you (do does did) after class today?

   After _____

3. Why (are is) you (study studies studying) English now?

   I _____

4. What (do you like you like) to do when you (have has) free time?

   When _____

Exercise 5

Write sentences.

1. dog / often / walk in a circle / before / lie down

   _____

   _____

2. next year / after / we / get married / live / apartment

   _____

   _____

3. yesterday, I / can't / go swim / because / pool / closed

   _____

   _____

4. she / very surprised / when / she / win / lottery

   _____

   _____

5. when / Carlos / nervous / he / always / bite / lip

   _____

   _____

6. I / stop / chew / gum / because / it / gave / headaches

   _____

   _____

Discuss

a. Do you have a dog? If yes, does it walk in a circle before it lies down?

b. Do you like to swim? Where do you swim?

c. Did you ever win the lottery? Did you ever win anything? When?

d. Are any of your friends going to get married soon? If yes, when?

e. What do you do when you are nervous?

f. Do you chew gum? If yes, when do you chew it?

Exercise 6

Complete each sentence with the correct word from the list.

after	because	before	when

1. It's a good idea to look both ways _____ you cross the street.

2. Why did he get the job? He got the job _____ he has the right skills.

3. For best results, read the directions _____ you start the test.

4. My son is planning to go to college _____ high school.

5. _____ you have time to get together again, call me.

6. Why was she late? She was late _____ she got lost in the city.

7. Close the door behind you _____ you leave the room.

8. _____ you drink the soda, please recycle the soda can.

Discuss

a. When do you read directions?
b. Do you have a job? If yes, why did you get the job?
c. What are you planning to do after you complete this class?
d. What things do you recycle?

Exercise 7

Complete the sentences. Start with the names of people you know.
Then discuss with a partner.

1. _____ always _____ before class.

2. _____ never _____ after work.

3. Last night, _____ did not _____ because

    _____ .

4. When _____ was _____ years old, _____

    _____ .

Exercise 8

Write sentences with the words.

1. before I came to this city

   _____

   _____

2. after I finish studying English

   _____

   _____

3. because I am from

   _____

   _____

4. when I was a child

   _____

   _____

5. before

   _____

   _____

6. after

   _____

   _____

7. when

   _____

   _____

8. because

   _____

   _____

Past Progressive Tense

22

At 8:30 last night, we were playing basketball.

Past Progressive Verb Form

was/were + (verb + *-ing*)
Examples: I was working.
            They were sleeping.

Question

Was/Were + subject + (verb + *-ing*)
Examples: Was she studying?
            Where were you living?

Negative

was/were + *not* + (verb + *-ing*)
Examples: It was not raining.
            We were not watching TV.

Using the Past Progressive

The past progressive tense shows a continuous action. It can show an action that was in progress at the time something else happened.
Examples: In 2002, they were living in Europe.
Last night, I was sleeping when the phone rang.

While with the Past Progressive

while = during this time
Examples: While we were shopping, we saw our teacher.
While you were cooking dinner, I was studying.

Exercise 1: Dictation

Read the first sentence while your teacher reads it. Write the second sentence that the teacher reads.

1. Isabelle did not answer the telephone last night.

   _____

2. They live in London now.

   _____

3. It was difficult to study last Saturday.

   _____

4. They did not take the bus yesterday.

   _____

5. My friend had a bad accident.

   _____

Discuss
a. Did you talk on the phone with anyone last night?
b. Where do you live now? Where were you living two years ago?
c. What were you doing last Saturday at noon?
d. The last time you rode a bus, where was it going?
e. Were you ever in a car accident? What happened?

Exercise 2

Circle the correct words.

1. Last night (at on) 7:30, when the rain (start started starting),
   we (watch watched were watching) TV. We
   (not go did not go were not going) anywhere after that.

2. Yesterday afternoon, while Lily (is reading was reading reads) a
   story to her daughter, the little girl (fall fell were falling) asleep.

3. Mr. and Mrs. Martinez do not usually (go going) (shop shopping)
   together. Yesterday, while Mr. Martinez (visits was visiting visiting)
   his neighbors, Mrs. Martinez (goes going went) to the mall.

4. Last night, while Karl (studying was studied was studying), he
   (hears heard was heard) a strange noise, but it (is was were)
   only the wind.

Discuss

a. What were you doing last night at 7:30? Was it raining?
b. When you were a child, who read to you or told you stories?
c. When did you last go shopping?
   What happened while you were shopping?
d. What happened the last time you were studying?

Exercise 3

Fix any mistakes.

1. Last year at this time I going to school in my home country.

2. Last night, while they were sleeping, they felt an earthquake.

3. He was swimming when suddenly saw a shark.

4. The man was falling and was breaking his leg while he was skiing.

5. While we working on the computer, the power was going out.

Exercise 4

What were your classmates doing when the teacher came into class today? Use classmates' names and the past progressive.

1. _Yumiko was studying_ _____ when the teacher arrived.

2. _____ when the teacher entered the room.

3. _____ when the teacher walked in.

4. When the teacher arrived, _____ .

5. _____ and _____ _____
    when the teacher entered the classroom.

6. I _____ when the teacher came into class today.

Exercise 5

Write sentences. Use the past and past progressive tenses.

1. while / the girl / speak / she / begin / cry

    _____

2. while / I / visit / Paris / I / lose / passport

    _____

3. Mr. Lungu / cut / self / while / shave

    _____

4. Mr. Dosa / exercise / when he / have / heart attack

    _____

Discuss

a. When was the last time you cried?
b. Did you ever lose something important? If yes, when?
c. Were you on time today, or were you running late? Why?
d. What are you doing for exercise these days?

Exercise 6

Use the past tense to complete the sentences. Then combine the ideas in a sentence using *while* or *when*.

1. We ___began___ to eat dinner at 6:30 p.m.
   (begin)

   The phone ___rang___ at 6:33.
   (ring)

   ___While we were eating, the phone rang.___

   (or)

   ___We were eating when the phone rang.___

2. Rachel _____ to walk to school at 8:00 a.m.
   (begin)

   On the way to school, she _____ an accident.
   (see)

   While _____.

3. My friend and I _____ watching the movie at 9:00 p.m.
   (start)

   Before the movie ended, a chair _____ fire in the theater.
   (catch)

   We _____.

4. My mother _____ shopping at 3:00 p.m.
   (go)

   She _____ an old friend in one of the stores.
   (meet)

   While _____.

5. The two men _____ yesterday.
   (talk)

   At the same time, their dogs _____ in the yard.
   (play)

   While _____.

6. We _____ taking the test at 10:00.
   (start)

   My cell phone _____ at 10:25, before we finished.
   (ring)

   We _____.

Discuss

a. What did you see while you were coming to school today?

b. When did you last see a movie? What happened while you were watching?

c. Do you have a pet? If yes, what does it do while you are studying?

Exercise 7

Complete the questions and write answers. Discuss with a partner.

1. What _____ 1:00 a.m. last night?
   (you / doing)

   _____

2. Where _____ when they first met?
   (your parents / living)

   _____

3. What _____ when the sun rose this morning?
   (you / doing)

   _____

4. What did you see while you _____ school today?
   (come)

   _____

5. What do you usually do while _____ a car?
   (you / riding)

   _____

6. What _____ a few minutes ago?
   (your teacher / doing)

   _____

7. Where _____ this time last year?
   (you / living)

   _____

Exercise 8

Complete the sentences with your ideas. Use the past progressive.

1. Last Friday night at 9:30, my friends _____.

2. Last year at this time, I _____.

3. Last week at this time, we _____.

4. In 2001, my family _____.

5. Last night, while you _____, I _____.

Exercise 9

Write questions and answers.

1. _____
   (why / you / not play / soccer yesterday)

   _____
   (cannot play / because / working)

2. _____
   (why / Angela / not come / movie last Sunday)

   _____
   (visit / aunt and uncle all weekend)

3. _____
   (why / you late for work today)

   _____
   (have / flat tire / while / drive / work)

4. _____
   (why / the teacher / get upset yesterday)

   _____
   (some students / talk / while she / talk)

5. _____
   (why / you / not come / party last Friday)

   _____
   (I / take / care of my sick dog all night)

6. _____
   (why / you / not move last year)

   _____
   (I / planning / move, but / change / mind)

7. _____
   (why / Danielle / quit / her job)

   _____
   (hoping / get / promotion, but / not get it)

8. _____
   (why / you / leave / the party early)

   _____
   (leave / because / not feeling / well)

9. _____
   (what / you doing / yesterday)

   _____
   (all day yesterday / I / try / fix / car)

10. _____
    (what / happen / to your hand)

    _____
    (I / burn / while / fry / some vegetable)

Exercise 10

Write sentences with the words and your own ideas.

1. while / was watching

_____

2. fell / when

_____

3. was driving / when

_____

4. while / were playing

_____

5. found / while

_____

6. were listening / while

_____

7. when / was reading

_____

8. began / while

_____

9. were working / when

_____

Past Tense of Irregular Verbs

1

Present	Past	Present	Past
begin	began	lose	lost
break	broke	make	made
bring	brought	meet	met
build	built	put	put
buy	bought	read	read (/red/)
can	could	ride	rode
catch	caught	ring	rang
choose	chose	run	ran
come	came	quit	quit
cost	cost	say	said (/sed/)
cut	cut	see	saw
do	did	sell	sold
drink	drank	send	sent
drive	drove	set	set
eat	ate	shoot	shot
fall	fell	shut	shut
feel	felt	sing	sang
fight	fought	sit	sat
find	found	sleep	slept
fly	flew	speak	spoke
forget	forgot	spend	spent
get	got	stand	stood
give	gave	steal	stole
go	went	swim	swam
grow	grew	take	took
have	had	teach	taught
hear	heard	tell	told
hit	hit	think	thought
hold	held	throw	threw
hurt	hurt	understand	understood
keep	kept	wake	woke
know	knew	wear	wore
leave	left	win	won
let	let	write	wrote

2 Verb + Infinitive and Verb + Gerund

Verb + Infinitive (*to* + verb)

These verbs are often followed by an infinitive:

agree	hope	plan	tell
decide	learn	promise	try
expect	need	refuse	want
forget	offer	seem	would like

Example: They agreed to do business.

Verb + Gerund (verb + *-ing*)

These verbs are often followed by a gerund:

be afraid of	deny	finish	practice	talk about
be interested in	discuss	keep	quit	think about
consider	enjoy	keep on	stop	

Example: He enjoys playing soccer.

Verb + Infinitive or Gerund

These verbs are often followed by either an infinitive verb
or a gerund:

begin	like
continue	love
hate	start

Example: It began to rain. (or) It began raining.

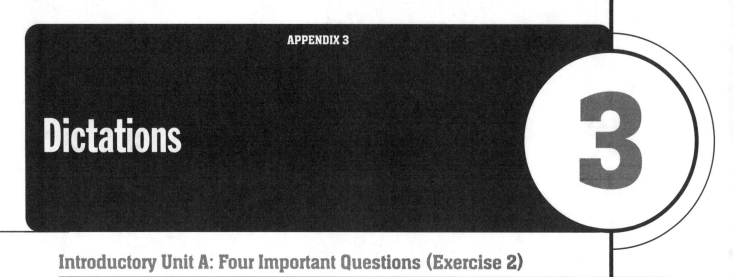

Dictations

Introductory Unit A: Four Important Questions (Exercise 2)

1. whale
2. bird
3. monkey
4. snake
5. turtle

Introductory Unit B: Parts of Speech and Sentence Structure (Exercise 1)

1. they
2. read
3. from
4. expensive
5. shoes
6. is
7. sit
8. nice
9. he
10. in

Review Unit A: Present-Tense Verbs (Exercise 1)

1. Japan is an island.
2. Japanese people often eat fish for dinner.
3. There are a lot of banks in Tokyo.
4. Japan does not have much oil.

Review Unit B: Present-Tense Questions (Exercise 1)

1. How old is your best friend?
2. What time do you usually get up on weekdays?
3. Are you quiet or talkative?
4. How many desks are there in your classroom?
5. Who in the class has a car?

Review Unit B: Present-Tense Questions (Exercise 8)

1. What is your name?
2. Where are you from?
3. What languages do you speak?
4. How old are you?
5. When is your birthday?
6. Are you married or single?
7. Where do you live?
8. Who lives with you?
9. Why are you studying English here?
10. What do you do in your free time?

Unit 1: Prepositions of Time (Exercise 1)

1. afternoon
2. April
3. 7:30 p.m.
4. the morning
5. 1999
6. night
7. tonight
8. spring
9. August first
10. noon
11. Wednesday
12. weekend
13. every day
14. October 15, 2002

Unit 2: Prepositions of Place (Exercise 1)

1. The story starts on page 19.
2. My car is in the garage.
3. Taiwan is not far from China.
4. I'm not at home now.
5. Every morning, he reads the news on the Internet.

Unit 3: Count and Noncount Nouns and Modifiers (Exercise 1)

1. Chinese food is popular around the world.
2. Every day, she wears a different dress.
3. I don't have any time today.
4. He drinks two cups of coffee in the morning.
5. Because of the buses, there is a lot of traffic in the city.
6. Children need a lot of love.

Unit 4: Object Pronouns (Exercise 1)

1. Donald loves Susanna.
   Donald loves her.
2. The teacher has the books.
   The teacher has them.
3. The children are with their mother.
   The children are with her.
4. Maria and I sit next to Bob.
   Maria and I sit next to him.
5. Mrs. Smith knows my friend and me.
   Mrs. Smith knows us.

Unit 5: Comparative and Superlative Adjectives (Exercise 1)

1. big
2. long
3. easy
4. good
5. intelligent
6. dirty
7. tired
8. important
9. cheap
10. hot

Unit 6: Modals: *Can, Might, Should, Must* (Exercise 1)

1. Children must not play with matches.
2. Parents should teach their children right from wrong.
3. It might be hot tomorrow.
4. Many people in Holland can speak English.

Unit 7: Adverbs (Exercise 1)

1. slowly
2. careful
3. softly
4. heavy
5. politely
6. easily
7. fast
8. well
9. completely

Unit 8: Present Progressive Tense (Exercise 1)

1. The teacher is reading right now.
2. The class always begins at _____ o'clock.
3. We are not taking a test now.
4. She understands the grammar now.
5. What is [student's name] doing now?
6. We don't have homework every night.

Unit 9: Future Tense (Exercise 1)

1. We're going to have a picnic on Saturday. Can you come?
2. Tina won't be here tomorrow. She has a doctor's appointment.
3. I'm not going to take classes next year. I'm going to work full time.
4. My neighbor is going to move soon. He's going to sell his house.
5. Please come over for dinner tomorrow night. You'll love my cooking.
6. Are you going to go to the library tonight? How long will you stay?

Unit 10: Sentences with *If* Clauses (Exercise 2)

1. John exercises every day if he has time.
2. If you need a ride, call me.
3. Students shouldn't come to school if they are sick.
4. If there is another war, many people will die.

Unit 11: Forms of *Other* (Exercise 1)

1. There are many countries in Central America. Honduras is one, and Guatemala is another.
2. Tuna is a kind of fish. Other kinds of fish are salmon and halibut.
3. California has three big cities on the coast. One is Los Angeles, and the others are San Diego and San Francisco.
4. The Japanese flag has only two colors. One is white, and the other is red.

Unit 12: Past Tense of the Verb *Be* (Exercise 1)

1. Last night at 8:00, we weren't at home. We were at a party.
2. Why were you angry yesterday?
3. Nadine was a good tennis player in school, but she doesn't play now.
4. How long was the movie?
5. Mr. Carera was a businessman for many years, but now he is retired.

Unit 13: *There Was* and *There Were* (Exercise 1)

1. In 1998, there was a lot of rain in Europe.
2. Last Friday, there were more than 100 people at the party.
3. Every day, there are many children at the park.
4. There was no time to call you yesterday.
5. There were not any American students in my school.

Unit 14: Past Tense of Regular Verbs (Exercise 1)

1. pull
2. work
3. stay
4. need
5. try
6. die
7. like
8. stop

Unit 15: Past Tense of Irregular Verbs 1 (Exercise 1)

1. I bought this book at the bookstore.
2. The teacher did not run to class today.
3. Last week, we saw a movie in class.
4. No one came on time today.
5. We had a test yesterday.
6. One student made cookies for the class.
7. The teacher said "Good morning" to us.

Unit 16: Past Tense of Irregular Verbs 2 (Exercise 1)

1. I understood yesterday's lesson very well.
2. Last week, he did not ride his bike to school because it was cold.
3. She paid $75 for her new camera.
4. They met seven years ago at a party.
5. Last night, we heard some strange noises outside.

Unit 17: Past Tense of Irregular Verbs 3 (Exercise 1)

1. Yesterday's class began a few minutes late.
2. I usually choose vanilla ice cream, but last night I chose chocolate.
3. The boxer fought hard, but he could not win his match.
4. The boy hurt his knee, so his sister put a bandage on it.
5. My mother taught me to swim, and I swam every day when I was young.
6. On my last birthday, my friends brought a cake and sang a song for me.

Unit 18: Past-Tense Questions (Exercise 1)

1. Did you walk to class today?
2. How was the weather last Saturday?
3. How much did your lunch cost yesterday?
4. Were you home at 9:00 last night?

Unit 19: Verb + Infinitive and Verb + Gerund (Exercise 1)

1. He plans to get another job.
2. We are trying to learn some new grammar.
3. My class does not like doing homework.
4. Our teacher forgot to give us homework last night.
5. We do not enjoy taking tests.
6. I am thinking about studying another language after English.
7. I want to go to the movies tonight.

Unit 20: The Definite Article *The* (Exercise 1)

1. Earth is the third planet from the sun.
2. We went to a baseball game. During the game, it started to rain.
3. The country north of the United States is Canada.
4. The first day of the week in many countries is Sunday.
5. Whales are not fish. They are mammals.

Unit 21: Connecting Words: *Before, After, When, Because* (Exercise 1)

1. Many people wear glasses when they read or drive.
2. They wear glasses because their eyes are not strong.
3. Some people must get glasses before they can get a driver's license.
4. After my friend reads for a long time, his eyes are very tired.

Unit 22: Past Progressive Tense (Exercise 1)

1. Isabelle did not answer the telephone last night. She was sleeping when I called her.
2. They live in London now. Two years ago, they were living in New York.
3. It was difficult to study last Saturday. While I was studying, my neighbors were having a party.
4. They did not take the bus yesterday. A friend offered them a ride while they were waiting at the bus stop.
5. My friend had a bad accident. He was driving very fast when he hit another car.

Grammar Handbook

Introductory Unit A : Four Important Questions

Ways to ask the questions

Meaning: What does _____ mean?
(or)
What is the meaning of _____?

Spelling: How do you spell _____?
(or)
What is the spelling of _____?

Pronunciation: How do you pronounce _____?
(or)
What is the pronunciation of _____?

Translation: How do you say _____ in (language)?

Learn the questions correctly!

Incorrect: ~~What means *plum*?~~
~~How you spell *strawberry*?~~

Correct: What does *plum* mean?
How do you spell *strawberry*?

Introductory Unit B: Parts of Speech and Sentence Structure

Nouns name people, places, things, or ideas. Here are some nouns.

baby	football	information	school
desk	happiness	king	stamps
English	heart	medicine	swimming pool

Pronouns take the place of nouns.

Subject Pronouns		Object Pronouns	
I	we	me	us
you	you	you	you
he/she/it	they	him/her/it	them

Adjectives describe nouns.

Examples: cheap tickets   great game   scary movie
funny story   handsome man   short time
gray hair   married couple   spicy food

Prepositions show location, time, direction, or connection. These are some prepositions.

above	between	for	like	on	under
at	by	from	near	through	with
behind	during	in	of	to	

A prepositional phrase = preposition + noun (or) noun phrase.

Examples: by hand   during the day   between the two houses
from Italy   like my mother   behind the restaurant

Verbs include the verb *be* and other verbs. Verbs show being or action.

The verb *be* shows being. Here are the present-tense forms.

Singular	Plural
I am	we are
you are	you are
he/she/it is	they are

Examples: I am ready.
You are a good friend.
Frank is at work.
We are new students.
Video games are fun.

Other verbs show action. The actions may be physical, mental, or emotional. Here are some other verbs.

buy	do	find	love	need	open	say	understand	want

Examples: We buy groceries on Saturday.
I understand you.
He wants some money.

Basic sentence structure is subject + verb.
Some common sentence structures follow.

Subject (noun or pronoun) + verb (*be* or other verb)

Examples: I am from Poland.
The baby sleeps a lot.

Subject (noun or pronoun) + verb *be* + complement
(A complement may be a noun, adjective,
or prepositional phrase.)

Examples: Dr. Stevens is an engineer.
This soup is delicious.
They are in the living room.

Subject (noun or pronoun) + verb + object (noun or pronoun)
(or)
Subject (noun or pronoun) + verb + prepositional phrase

Examples: I like pizza.
Ellen works at the post office.

Sometimes in commands or requests the subject *you* is not stated.

Examples: Call me tomorrow.
Please open the door.

Review Unit A: Present-Tense Verbs

These are the present-tense forms of the verb *be*.

Affirmative	Negative
I am	I am not
you are	you are not
he/she/it is	he/she/it is not
we are	we are not
you are	you are not
they are	they are not

Examples: He is a music teacher.
(verb *be* + noun)

I am not ready.
(verb *be* + adjective)

The children are at home.
(verb *be* + prepositional phrase)

These are the present-tense forms of some other verbs.

Affirmative	Negative
I like	I do not like
you eat	you do not eat
he/she/it has	he/she/it does not have
we need	we do not need
you think	you do not think
they want	they do not want

Examples: I do not play the piano.
(verb + noun)

Bob studies at the library.
(verb + prepositional phrase)

She exercises every day.
(verb + time expression)

I never drink and drive.
(adverb of frequency + verb)

There is and there are express existence or location. Use there is with a singular subject. Use there are with a plural subject.

Affirmative	Negative		
There is	There is not	(or)	There isn't
There are	There are not	(or)	There aren't

Examples: There is a famous museum in Paris.
There are no classes on Sunday.
There aren't any classes on Sunday.

Review Unit B: Present-Tense Questions

Yes/no and or questions with the verb be take the form verb be + subject.

Am I . . . ?	Are we . . . ?
Are you . . . ?	Are you . . . ?
Is he/she/it . . . ?	Are they . . . ?

Examples: Is your name common in your country? Yes, it is (or) No, it isn't.
Are you from China or Korea? I'm from Korea.

Wh- questions with the verb be take the form wh- question word + verb be + subject.

Examples: What city are you from? I'm from Seoul.
Why is she late? She's late because her car has a flat tire.

Is there/Are there questions take the forms
Is there + singular subject/**Are there** + plural subject.

> *Examples:* Is there a bus stop near here?   Yes, there is. (or) No, there isn't.
> Are there buses after 11:00?   Yes, there are. (or) No, there aren't.

How many . . . are there . . . ?

> *Examples:* How many students are there in your class? There are 17.

Yes/no and **or** questions with other verbs take the form **Do/Does** +
subject + simple form of the verb.

> Do I need . . . ?   Do we have . . . ?
> Do you know . . . ?   Do you need . . .?
> Does he/she/it have . . .? Do they want . . .?
> *Examples:* Do you know Halim? Yes, I do. (or) No, I don't.
> Does he have black or brown hair? He has black hair.

Wh- questions with other verbs take the form
wh- question word + **do/does** + subject + verb.

> *Examples:* What languages do you speak? I speak Arabic and French.
> Where does she live? She lives near the mall.

If the question word is the subject or part of the subject, do not use
do/does. Use the form question word + verb.

> *Examples:* Who lives here? My roommate and I live here.
> How many people live here? Only two people live here.

Unit 1: Prepositions of Time

Use different prepositions with different time expressions.

Use *at* for a specific time.

> *Examples:* at 1 a.m., at noon

Use *on* for specific days or dates.

> *Examples:* on Saturday, on September 21, on the weekend,
> on the first day of class

Use *in* for a specific month, year, season, or time of day.

> *Examples:* in January, in 1997, in the winter, in the morning,
> in the afternoon, in the evening
> *Exception:* at night

Use *on* for a combination of day and time of day.

> *Examples:* on Friday night, on Monday mornings

Use *during* to mean within a period of time.

Examples: They take a vacation during the summer.
(= at some time within the summer)

He wrote the story during 1975.
(= at some time within 1975)

My son got sick during the night.
(= at some time within the night)

Certain time expressions take no prepositions.

Examples: **Now** I live away from my home.
We study **every day.**
Do we have a quiz **today?**
There is a party **tonight.**
Last Monday she was absent.
My birthday is **next week.**

Note the meaning of the plural form of days.

On Saturdays, they play soccer. = Every Saturday, they play soccer.
I call my family on Sundays. = Every Sunday, I call my family.

Prepositional phrases can come at the beginning, middle, or end of a sentence. Note comma use.

Examples: On the weekend, I go shopping with my sister.
I go shopping on the weekend with my sister.
I go shopping with my sister on the weekend.

Unit 2: Prepositions of Place

Use different prepositions with different types of places.

Use *in* with cities, states or regions, and countries.

Examples: in London, in Colorado, in the Northeast, in China

Use *in* to mean inside a place, room, or object.

Examples: The milk is in the refrigerator.
Michael is in his office.
I'll meet you in the supermarket. (inside the store)

Use *on* to mean "on top of" or "on the surface of."

Examples: Put it on my desk.
The exercise is on page 13.
There's a lot of dirt on my car.

Use *on* with streets and electronic media (TV, radio, Internet, etc.), including the telephone.

> *Examples:* I live on Cherry Street.
> We listen to music on the radio.
> I'm on the phone. (talking on the telephone)

Use *at* with specific addresses.

> *Example:* The house is at 241 Rosewood Street.

Use *at* for general location, especially for large places, for example, *store*, *school*, *home*, or *work* (workplace).

> *Examples:* On weekdays, there are many students at the library.
> I see my friends at school.
> They're always at home in the evening.

Use *to* for movement, often with verbs like *come* and *go*.

> *Examples:* Many students go to parties on Friday nights.
> Please come to class on time!
> *Exceptions:* Please come home now.
> Every winter, we go on vacation.

Other prepositions of place

above	between	in front of	next to
behind	far from	near	under

> *Example:* I live near the bank.

Some prepositions have the same meaning.

> over = above
> under = below
> behind = in back of
> near = close to
> *Example:* The post office is near the bank. = The post office is close to the bank.

Unit 3: Count and Noncount Nouns and Modifiers

Count nouns refer to things that can be counted.

> *Examples:* 1 chair—2 chairs—3 chairs
> one car—two cars—three cars
> a friend—some friends—a lot of friends

Noncount nouns refer to things that cannot be counted.

> *Examples:* water, love, advice

Noncount nouns are used for
> abstract ideas, such as *happiness* and *knowledge*
> liquids, such as *water* and *alcohol*
> gases, such as *air* and *oxygen*
> metals, such as *gold* and *silver*
> things that you cannot touch, such as *love* and *information*
> some kinds of food, such as *meat* and *rice*
> emotions, such as *fear* and *anger*
> group words, such as *fruit* and *furniture*
> things too numerous to count, such as *hair* and *sand*

Count nouns can have singular or plural forms.
> *Examples:* a book—books—four books
> his computer—some computers—50 computers
> the student—many students—2,000 students

Noncount nouns are always in a singular form.
> *Examples:* tea, some information, a lot of time

Be careful! Some nouns seem countable but are really noncount.
> *Example:* money (We say, "Count your money," but we can't say "one money, two moneys.")

A noncount noun can often be combined with a count noun.
> *Examples:* water—a glass of water—two cups of water
> advice—a piece of advice

Some noncount nouns name a group or category.
Compare these examples.

Noncount Terms	Related Count Nouns
furniture	a chair
jewelry	two rings
fruit	some apples

Do not use the article *a/an* with noncount nouns.
> *Incorrect:* ~~an air, a sand~~
> *Correct:* air—some air
> sand—a lot of sand

Use *some* and *any* with both count and noncount nouns.
Some and *any* are followed by a singular noncount noun
or by a plural count noun.
> *Examples:* some coffee, some friends
> any help, any cities

Use *much* with singular noncount nouns. Use *many* with plural count nouns. The expression *a lot of* (meaning "many" or "much") can be used with singular noncount nouns or plural count nouns.

> *Examples:* much homework, many friends
> a lot of homework, a lot of friends

Some nouns are both count and noncount.

> *Examples:* I have been to Europe many times. (count)
> I don't have much time today. (noncount)

Some common noncount nouns

advice	hair	peace
air	health	pollution
alcohol	help	rain
bread	history	rice
clothing	homework	sand
coffee	information	smoke
education	knowledge	snow
English	light	sugar
food	love	tea
fruit	luck	time
fun	meat	traffic
furniture	money	weather
garbage	music	work
gold	news	
grammar	noise	

Unit 4: Object Pronouns

Object pronouns are the object forms of subject pronouns.

Subject Pronouns		Object Pronouns	
I	we	me	us
you	you	you	you
he/she/it	they	him/her/it	them

Object pronouns come after a verb or a preposition. Object pronouns receive the action in a sentence.

> *Examples:* The teacher helps us.
> I live with them.
> This is for you.
> Give it to me.

Object pronouns are different from possessive adjectives
(my, your, his, her, its, our, their). Possessive adjectives are followed
by nouns or noun phrases. Object pronouns are not followed
immediately by nouns.

> ***Examples:*** I like his car.
> (possessive adjective *his,* object *car*)
>
> I like it.
> (object pronoun *it*)
>
> Wait for our teacher.
> (possessive adjective *our,* object *teacher*)
>
> Wait for her.
> (object pronoun *her*)

Unit 5: Comparative and Superlative Adjectives

Use the comparative form to compare two things or two sets of things.

Adjective	Comparative
small	smaller
big	bigger
intelligent	more intelligent

> ***Examples:*** A horse is bigger than a mouse.
> Monkeys are more intelligent than cows.
> Senegal is smaller than Sudan and Kenya.

**Use the superlative form to compare more than two things or to show
that one thing is different from all others in some way.**

Adjective	Comparative	Superlative
big	bigger	the biggest
difficult	more difficult	the most difficult

> ***Examples:*** Blue whales are the biggest animals.
> He has the most difficult job in this company.

Use *than* when a second item follows a comparative adjective.

> ***Example:*** A bicycle is cheaper than a car.

Normally, use *the* with superlatives.

> ***Example:*** February is the shortest month in the year.

**The form of comparative and superlative adjectives depends
on the length and spelling of the adjective.**

For adjectives with one syllable, add -er to form the comparative. Add -est to form the superlative.

Examples: fast—faster—the fastest
cheap—cheaper—the cheapest

For adjectives with two or more syllables, use *more* to form the comparative. Use *most* to form the superlative.

Examples: common—more common—the most common
difficult—more difficult—the most difficult
intelligent—more intelligent—the most intelligent

For adjectives with two syllables ending in *y*, to form the comparative, change the *y* to *i* and add -er. To form the superlative, change the *y* to *i* and add -est.

Examples: happy—happier—the happiest
dirty—dirtier—the dirtiest

Irregular adjectives are adjectives that do not follow these rules. Here are some common irregular adjectives.

good—better—the best
bad—worse—the worst
far—farther—the farthest

Unit 6: Modals: *Can, Might, Should, Must*

Modals are used with verbs. They can be used in affirmative statements, negative statements, and questions.

Affirmative: can play, might rain, should go, must study
Negative: cannot play, might not rain, should not go, must not forget
Questions: Can you play the piano? Should we go out or stay home?

The modals have different meanings.

can	=	is able to; has permission to
might	=	it's possible; maybe
should	=	it's advisable; it's the right thing to do
must	=	it's necessary
must not	=	it's prohibited, forbidden

Examples: Martin plays piano every day. He can play very well.
You cannot smoke in a hospital.
Where is my umbrella? It might rain today.
We have a big test tomorrow. We should not go out tonight.
You must not forget the meeting. You have to remember it!

The modals *may* and *could* also express possibility. *Have to* is also a common way to express necessity.

The form of the modal does not change for different subjects.
   Example: I can play the piano, and he can play, too.

Do not use *to* after the modal.
   Incorrect: ~~They should not to go.~~
   Correct: They should not go.

The modal is followed by a verb, not an adjective.
   Incorrect: ~~It might hot tomorrow.~~
   Correct: It might be hot tomorrow.

The negative form is modal + *not* + verb.
(Note that *cannot* is one word.)
   Examples: We must not forget.
             He cannot go. (or) He can't go.

The question form is modal + subject + verb.
   Examples: Can I use your pen?
             Where should we go for dinner?

Unit 7: Adverbs

Adjectives and adverbs have similar forms but different functions.
An adjective describes a noun. An adverb usually modifies a verb.
It tells how, when, or where something happens.
Examples: She is a quick runner.
         (*Quick* is an adjective. It describes the noun *runner*.)

   She runs quickly.
   (*Quickly* is an adverb. It modifies the verb *run*. The adverb *quickly* tells how she runs.)

   John is always careful.
   (*Careful* is an adjective. It describes the noun *John*.)

   John writes carefully.
   (*Carefully* is an adverb. It modifies the verb *writes*. It tells how he writes.)

Adverbs usually follow verbs. An object or prepositional phrase may come between a verb and its adverb.
   Example: He drives dangerously.
         He drives his car dangerously.
         He walks to school frequently. (or) He frequently walks to school.

Many adjectives can be changed to adverbs by adding *-ly*:

Adjectives	Adverbs
quick	quickly
careful	carefully

Some adjectives cannot be changed to adverbs.

Adjective	Adverb
big	~~bigly~~
small	~~smally~~

Some adjectives and their *-ly* adverbs have different meanings.

Adjective	Adverb
late	lately (means "recently")
hard	hardly (means "almost not")

Some adverbs are irregular.

good—well
fast—fast
hard—hard
early—early

Examples: She is a good basketball player. She plays basketball well.
This is a hard job. You have to work hard.

**If an adjective ends in *-y*, to form the adverb,
change the *y* to *i* and add *-ly*.**

Examples: happy—happily
noisy—noisily

Some adjectives end in *-ly*. They don't have adverb forms.

Examples: lovely, friendly, deadly, lively

The comparative form of an adverb = *more* + adverb.
The superlative form of an adverb = *most* + adverb.

Examples: I walk slowly.
He walks more slowly.
She walks the most slowly.

These are some common adverbs.

carefully	directly	hard	noisily	quietly	softly
completely	easily	heavily	politely	safely	well
correctly	fast	legally	privately	seriously	
dangerously	happily	loudly	quickly	slowly	

The simple present form of verb expresses a habitual action, something that happens regularly.

Example: We read every day.

The present progressive form of the verb expresses something that is in progress at the moment, something that is happening right now.

Example: We are reading right now.

The affirmative form of the present progressive is verb *be* + (verb + *-ing*).

Example: I am studying grammar now.

The negative form of the present progressive is verb *be* + *not* + (verb + *-ing*).

Example: I am not studying math.

The form of a question in the present progressive is verb *be* + subject + (verb + *-ing*).

Example: Are you studying math or grammar now?

The verb *be* is never followed by the simple form of the verb.

Incorrect: They ~~are listen~~ to the teacher now.
Correct: They are listening to the teacher.

Use the simple present with frequency words, like *always, usually, often, sometimes, never,* and *every day.* Use the present progressive with time words like *now, this week, this year,* and *today.*

Examples: We usually do homework at night. (simple present)
            We are not doing homework right now. (present progressive, negative)

Compare these examples.

Examples: I often read newspapers. (simple present)
            I am reading a book right now. (present progressive)

            I play baseball every Saturday. (simple present)
            This week, I'm not playing baseball. (present progressive)

            She never wears shorts. (simple present)
            She is wearing jeans today. (present progressive)

            It does not rain much in the desert. (simple present)
            It is not raining right now. (present progressive)

We sometimes study together. (simple present)
We are studying English this year. (present progressive)

They watch TV in the evening. (simple present)
They are not watching TV now. (present progressive)

Some verbs are not usually used in the present progressive, even when the sentence is about something happening right now. Here are some of these verbs:

believe	have	know	love	remember	understand
forget	hear	like	need	see	want

Examples: I have two cars now.
Now he understands completely.
We do not need a new computer right now.
Do you remember me?

Unit 9: Future Tense

There are two common forms for the future: *will* + verb and *be* + *going to* + verb.
Examples: Tomorrow, my plane will leave at 7:00 a.m.
Next summer, he is going to return to his country.

Often, *will* and *be going to* can be used interchangeably.
Examples: Next weekend, the beach will be crowded.
Next weekend, the beach is going to be crowded.

Will is a modal. It does not change form. It is followed by the simple form of the verb.
Examples: He will move to another city next year. His girlfriend
will move, too.

The verb *be* in *be going to* changes according to person and number. *Be going to* is followed by the base form of the verb.
Examples: I am going to graduate next May.
My husband is going to graduate also.
We are going to take a vacation after that.

Will and *be going to* are sometimes followed by the verb *be* + adjective.
Examples: It will be hot next summer.
They are going to be tired after the game.
The test tomorrow will be difficult.

The question forms are *will* + subject + verb
and *be* + subject + *going to* + verb.

    Examples: Will you be home tonight at 9:00?
                When will the party start?
                Are you going to be home tonight at 9:00?
                When is the party going to start?

The negative forms are *will not (won't)* + verb
and *be not going to* + verb.

    Examples: They will not (won't) have enough time to finish.
                It is not going to rain tomorrow.

These are some common future time words.

    in   next   soon   this   tomorrow
    Examples: We will do it next week.
                They are going to arrive in two days.
                The weather will soon change.
                Tomorrow, I am going to stay home.
                I am going to study this weekend.

No prepositions are used with the time expressions *next, soon, this,*
and *tomorrow.*

    Example: The game will be this weekend.

Some verbs can express the future with the simple present.

    arrive   be   begin   close   end   leave   open
    Examples: Her plane arrives at 11:00 a.m. this Thursday.
                The movie begins tonight at 7:30.
                The test is at 8:00 tomorrow.

Many verbs can express the future with the present progressive.

    arrive   come   fly   have   take   work
    begin   do   go   move   walk
    Examples: They are going to the mountains next weekend.
                We're flying to Spain next month.
                I'm having a party this Friday.

Unit 10: Sentences with *If* Clauses

If **sentences have two clauses: the *if* clause (*if* + subject + verb)**
and the main clause (subject + verb).

    Example: If I need help, I will call you.
              I'll call you if I need help.

When the *if* clause begins the sentence, use a comma to separate it from the main clause.

> *Example:* If I pass the driving test, I will get my driver's license.

When the *if* clause comes after the main clause, no comma is necessary.

> *Example:* I will get my driver's license if I pass the driving test.

An *if* sentence can refer to the present or the future.

> *Present:* If you are tired now, you shouldn't drive.
> *Future:* If it rains tomorrow, we will stay home.

To express future time with *if,* use the present tense in the *if* clause and the future tense in the main clause.

> *Incorrect:* ~~If we will have time tomorrow, we will go to a movie.~~
> *Correct:* If we have time tomorrow, we will go to a movie.

Modals are often used in *if* sentences.

> *Example:* If you have a problem, I can help you.
> You should not eat a lot of red meat if you want a healthy heart.

If indicates possibility, so *might* is not usually used in an *if* clause. *Might* is used in the main clause.

> *Examples:* I might work tomorrow. If I work tomorrow, I will be very tired.
> If you drive too fast, you might get a ticket.

Unit 11: Forms of *Other*

There are several forms of the word *other:*

> *Singular:* another, the other
> *Plural:*   other, others, the other, the others

Another is always singular. *Another* can be used alone or followed by a singular noun. *Another* means, "There are more. There are others. The list is not finished."

> *Examples:* Japanese is an Asian language. Korean is another.
> Japanese is an Asian language. Korean is another Asian language.
> (Both examples mean, "There are more Asian languages. The list of Asian languages is not finished.")

The other can be used alone or followed by a singular noun.
The other means, "There are no more. There are no others.
The list is finished."

  Examples: There are two official languages in Canada. One is English, and the
  other is French.
  There are two official languages in Canada. One language is
  English, and the other language is French.
  (Both examples mean, "There are no other official languages in
  Canada. The list of official languages in Canada is finished.")

Other is followed by a plural noun. **Other** means, "There are more.
There are others. The list is not finished."

  Example: Elephants are one kind of animal. Eagles and snakes are other kinds.
  (This means, "There are other kinds of animals. The list of animals is
  not finished.")

Others is plural. **Others** is used alone; it is not followed by a noun.
Others means, "There are more. There are others. The list is not
finished."

  Example: Elephants are one kind of animal. Others are eagles and snakes.
  (This means, "There are more kinds of animals, like cats and fish.
  The list of animals is not finished.")

The other can be followed by a singular or plural noun.
The other + plural noun means, "There are no more.
There are no others. The list is finished."

  Example: There are five elephants at the zoo. Two are African elephants, with
  big ears, and the other elephants are Indian elephants, with small ears.
  (This means, "There are no more elephants at the zoo. There are no
  others. The list of elephants at the zoo is finished.")

The others is plural. **The others** is not followed by a noun. **The others**
means, "There are no more. There are no others. The list is finished."

  Example: There are five elephants at the zoo. Two are African elephants, and
  the others are Indian elephants.
  (This means, "There are no more elephants at the zoo. There are no
  others. The list is finished.")

Do not use a noun after *others*.
  Incorrect: ~~Some people like coffee, and others people like tea.~~
  Correct: Some people like coffee, and others like tea.

Another is never followed by a plural noun.

Incorrect: ~~Some people like coffee, and another people like tea.~~

Correct: Some people like coffee, and other people like tea.

Unit 12: Past Tense of the Verb *Be*

Here are the past-tense forms of the verb *be*.

I was	we were
you were (singular)	you were (plural)
he/she/it was	they were

The verb *be* is often followed by adjectives, nouns, or prepositional phrases.

Examples: My first car was not expensive.
(*be* + adjective)

His mother was an actress in high school.
(*be* + noun)

They were at a party last night.
(*be* + prepositional phrase)

Questions use this form: *Wh*- question word + verb *be* + subject.

Incorrect: ~~Why you were late yesterday?~~

Correct: Why were you late yesterday?
Were they in class yesterday?
Where was your class last year?

Negatives use this form: *was/were* + not.

Examples: She was not upset about the news.
They were not ready.

Remember! Do not combine the verb *be* with *do/does*.

Incorrect: ~~Do you were absent yesterday?~~

Correct: Were you absent yesterday?

Some common past time expressions

last (time word)   (time word) ago   in (time word)   yesterday

Examples: last night, last week
four days ago, 10 years ago
in 2001, in the 19th century

There was and **There were** express past location, past events, or past existence.

> *Examples:* Yesterday there was money in the box, but today the box is empty.
>
> In 1989, there were many changes in the world.

There was is followed by a singular subject. **There were** is followed by a plural subject.

> *Examples:* Last night, there was a good movie on TV. (singular)
>
> Last week, there were two accidents on my street. (plural)

If there are two subjects, the number of the verb depends on the subject closest to the verb.

> *Examples:* Last semester, there was a student from Mexico and two students from Korea in my class.
>
> Last semester, there were two students from Korea and a student from Mexico in my class.

Questions use this form: *Was there/Were there.*

> *Examples:* Were there any Americans in your last class? No, there weren't.
>
> Was there a full moon last night? Yes, there was.

Negatives take these forms: *there was not/there were not* **or** *there was no/there were no.* **Different subject constructions can follow.**

> *Examples:* There was not a soccer game last weekend.
> (or)
> There was no soccer game last weekend.
> (subject = singular count noun)
>
> There was not any salt in the soup.
> (or)
> There was no salt in the soup.
> (subject = noncount noun)
>
> Yesterday, there were not any clouds in the sky.
> (or)
> Yesterday, there were no clouds in the sky.
> (subject = plural count noun)

There was and *There were* are different from *It was* and *They were.*
There was and *There were* express past location, events, or existence.
The words *it* and *they* normally refer to something mentioned previously.
> *Examples:* There was a party last night at my neighbor's house.
> It (the party) was very noisy.
> There were a lot of people at the party.
> They (the people) were very noisy.

There was and *There were* are not normally followed by *the.*
> *Incorrect:* ~~There was the refrigerator in my last apartment.~~
> *Correct:* There was a refrigerator in my last apartment.

There was and *There were* are usually followed by a noun
or noun phrase, not just an adjective.
> *Correct:* Ten years ago, there was a post office on this street.
> *Incorrect:* ~~There was very convenient.~~
> *Correct:* It was very convenient.

Unit 14: Past Tense of Regular Verbs

There are two kinds of verbs in English: regular and irregular.
To make the past tense of regular verbs, add *-ed* to the verb.
> *Example:* look—looked

Compare the verbs in these examples.
> *Examples:* Many Brazilians play soccer. (present tense, affirmative)
> I played tennis when I was a child. (past tense, affirmative)
>
> Do many Brazilians play baseball? (present tense, question)
> Did you play soccer last Saturday? (past tense, question)
>
> Most Brazilians do not play baseball. (present tense, negative)
> I did not play soccer last Saturday. (past tense, negative)

To form questions, use *did* and the simple form of the verb.
> *Example:* Did you play basketball last Saturday?
> Yes, I did. (or) No, I didn't.

The negative form is *did not (didn't)* + simple form of verb.
> *Incorrect:* ~~Last Saturday, I did not played soccer.~~
> *Correct:* Last Saturday, I did not play soccer.

The past-tense form of the verb is the same for all persons.
> *Examples:* I played, he played, you played, they played

With verbs ending in *y* preceded by a consonant, change the *y* to *i* and add *-ed* to form the past tense.
> ***Examples:*** carry—carried, study—studied

With one-syllable verbs ending in a single consonant (except *w, x,* or *y*) and preceded by a single vowel, double the final consonant and add *-ed* to form the past tense.
> ***Examples:*** plan—planned, stop—stopped, show—showed

With one-syllable verbs ending in a single consonant but preceded by two vowels, add *-ed* to form the past tense.
> ***Examples:*** clean—cleaned, look—looked

With verbs ending in *e* preceded by a consonant, add *-d* to form the past tense.
> ***Examples:*** race—raced, smile—smiled

With two-syllable verbs, if the accent is on the first syllable and the verb ends in a single consonant preceded by a single vowel, add *-ed* to form the past tense.
> ***Examples:*** happen—happened, listen—listened

With two-syllable verbs, if the accent is on the second syllable and the verb ends in a single consonant preceded by a single vowel, double the final consonant and add *-ed* to form the past tense.
> ***Examples:*** occur—occurred, prefer—preferred

Some other regular past-tense verbs have irregular spellings.
> ***Examples:*** pay—paid, say—said

Some common expressions used with the past tense are:
> (time) ago   in (past time)   last (time)   on (past time)   yesterday
> ***Examples:*** They lived here 5 years ago.
> I graduated in June 2000.
> The accident was on May 7, 2002.
> It ended last week.
> I walked to school yesterday.

Units 15, 16, and 17: Past Tense of Irregular Verbs

See Appendix 1 for a list of irregular verbs.

The form of an irregular verb in the past tense is the same for all persons. Compare the past tense forms of *go*.

Affirmative: I went, you went, she went, they went
Question: Did you go? Did she go? Did they go?
Negative: I did not go, we did not go, they did not go

Question form = *Did* + subject + simple form of the verb

Incorrect: ~~Did you saw the movie?~~
~~Were you buy anything?~~
~~Where he found that book?~~

Correct: Did you see the movie?
Did you buy anything?
Where did he find that book?

Negative form = *did not* + simple form of the verb

Incorrect: ~~They did not went shopping yesterday.~~
Correct: They did not go shopping yesterday.

Unit 18: Past-Tense Questions

***Yes/no* and *or* questions with the past tense of the verb *be*
= verb *be* + subject**

Was I . . .?   Were we . . .?
Were you . . .?   Were you . . .?
Was he/she/it . . .?   Were they . . .?

Examples: Was I right or wrong last night?
Were you sick yesterday?
Was he late or on time for yesterday's meeting?
Were we too noisy at last night's party?
Were those shoes cheap or expensive?

Short answers to *yes/no* questions

Affirmative	Negative
Yes, I was.	No, I wasn't.
Yes, you were.	No, you weren't.
Yes, we were.	No, we weren't.
Yes, he/she/it was.	No, he/she/it wasn't.
Yes, they were.	No, they weren't.

Examples: Was he angry? No, he wasn't.
Were your grades in school good? Yes, they were.

Wh- questions with the past tense of the verb *be*
= *Wh-* question word + verb *be* + subject

    Examples: When was your last vacation?

              Why were they late to yesterday's class?

              How much was your new computer?

Remember some *Wh-* question words.

How	Where	How many	What color
What	Who	How much	What kind
When	Why	How old	What time

Yes/no and *or* questions with other past-tense verbs
= *Did* + subject + simple form of verb

Did I get . . . ?	Did we win . . . ?
Did you do . . . ?	Did you see . . . ?
Did he go . . . ?	
Did Linda work . . . ?	Did they like . . . ?
Did it rain . . . ?	

    Examples: Did you do last night's homework?

              Did Linda work yesterday, or did she stay home?

              Did it rain last night?

              Did we win or lose the game?

Short answers to *yes/no* questions:

Yes, I did.	(or)	No, I didn't.
Yes, you did.	(or)	No, you didn't.
Yes, she did.	(or)	No, he didn't.
Yes, they did.	(or)	No, we didn't.

    Examples: Did he get a good grade? Yes, he did.

              Did it rain last night? No, it didn't.

Wh- questions with other past tense verbs
= *Wh-* question word + *did* + subject + simple form of verb

    Examples: Oh, why did I do that?

              Where did you put the money?

              Why didn't he come?

              How much did it cost?

              What time did they go home?

Sometimes a *Wh-* question word is the subject of the sentence. This structure = *Wh-* question word as subject + past tense of the verb.

    Examples: Who gave you that book?

              What happened to your radio?

The infinitive form is *to* + verb; the gerund form is the verb + *-ing.*

> *Examples:* to buy (infinitive)
> buying (gerund)

Certain verbs are followed by infinitives; other verbs are followed by gerunds. Some verbs can be followed by either an infinitive or a gerund.

> *Examples:* We need to buy a new computer.
> (verb *need* + infinitive *to buy*)
>
> He enjoys listening to music.
> (verb *enjoy* + gerund *listening*)
>
> They like to play soccer.
> (verb *like* + infinitive *to play*)
> (or)
> They like playing soccer.
> (verb *like* + gerund *playing*)

The main verb changes in tense and number.
The infinitive or gerund does not change.

> *Examples:* He wanted to move to another city, but now he plans to stay here.
> (past tense of verb *want* + infinitive *to move;*
> 3rd person singular, present tense of verb *plan* + infinitive *to stay*)
>
> They finished doing their homework at 12:00 last night.
> (past tense of verb *finish* + gerund *doing*)

To form the negative, use *not* + infinitive/gerund.

> *Examples:* She decided not to stay in the United States.
> I am thinking about not going to the party tomorrow.

Here are some common verbs followed by infinitives. Most are regular verbs with past tense ending in *-ed.* Irregular past-tense forms are shown in parentheses ( ).

agree	forget (forgot)	need	promise	tell (told)
decide	hope	offer	refuse	try
expect	learn	plan	seem	want

would like (modal verb; does not change)

> *Examples:* I refuse to quit.
> He is trying to spend more time with his family.
> I would like to find a cheaper apartment.

Note the following structure: verb + (someone) + infinitive
Examples: The teacher expects us to work hard.
We want our friends to visit us next summer.

Here are some common verbs and verb-preposition combinations followed by gerunds. Most are regular verbs with past tense ending in *-ed*. Irregular past-tense forms are shown in parentheses ( ).

consider	finish	keep—keep on (kept)	be (was/were) afraid of
deny	practice	talk about	be (was/were) interested in
discuss	quit (quit)	think (thought) about	
enjoy	stop		

Examples: She is considering changing her job.
I stopped worrying about so many things.

Use gerunds after prepositions.
Examples: He is interested in learning another language.
(preposition *in* followed by the gerund *learning*)

They are talking about moving to another city.
(preposition *about* followed by the gerund *moving*)

Use a gerund after the verb *go* to name many common activities, such as camping, fishing, hiking, sailing, shopping, surfing, and swimming.
Examples: Every summer, we go camping in the mountains.
Last weekend, we went shopping at the mall.

Here are some common verbs that can be followed by either an infinitive or gerund. Most are regular verbs with past tense ending in *-ed*. Irregular past-tense forms are shown in parentheses ( ).

begin (began)	continue	hate	like	love	start

Examples: It started to rain.　　(or)　　It started raining.
They continued talking.　　(or)　　They continued to talk.

Unit 20: The Definite Article *The*

The definite article in English is *the*. It has many uses.

Use *the* with something unique, the only one.
Examples: The King of Saudi Arabia lives in the capital, Riyadh.
(There is only one King of Saudi Arabia and only one capital.)

The sun is a star.
(There is only one sun, but there are many stars.)

The Sahara Desert is in Africa.
(There is only one desert named the Sahara Desert.)

The is often used with a noun that was already identified.
Normally, use *a/an* when you mention something the first time,
and after that, use *the*.

Examples: We had a test yesterday. After the test, we went to lunch together.
(The test was already identified as yesterday's test.)

I talked to a policeman. The policeman tried to help me.
(The policeman was already identified as the policeman I talked to.)

Use *the* with a noun that is identified or specified in some way.

Examples: Food is necessary to live.
(This refers to food in general.)

The food on the table is for dinner tonight.
The food in the refrigerator is for tomorrow.
(These examples refer to specific food in specific locations.)

Use *the* for the whole of a category or for all of the items in a category.

Examples: The desks in my class are hard. = all the desks in my class
The oceans contain many minerals. = all of the oceans

Use *the* to refer to a class of items.

Examples: The whale is the biggest animal in the world.
(*The whale* represents the whole class of whales.)

Edison invented the electric light.
(*The electric light* represents the class of invention, electric lights.)

Do NOT use *the* with the following kinds of nouns:

people's names:	Mrs. Smith; David
languages:	Spanish; Russian
countries:	China; Peru (exception: the United States)
U.S. states:	California; Arizona; Florida
cities:	Amsterdam; Seoul
planets:	Mars; Venus (exception: Earth or the Earth)
days of the week and months:	Sunday; December
names of streets:	Main Street; 1st Avenue
foods:	bananas; chicken
meals:	breakfast; lunch; dinner
academic subjects:	chemistry; math
materials:	plastic; metal; wood
some time expressions:	last year; next weekend
sports:	basketball; tennis

Use *the* with the following kinds of nouns and expressions:

rivers and oceans:	the Nile River; the Pacific Ocean
ordinal numbers as adjectives:	the first time; on the second day
with *same*:	at the same time; the same color
with some *of* phrases:	the top of the page; the music of the 60s
superlatives:	the biggest animal; the most expensive car
some countries:	the United States of America (the USA)

Do not use *the* for general statements.

> *Example:* Cars have four wheels.
> (cars in general; all cars)

Use *the* for something definite and specific.

> *Example:* The car in the garage is my father's.
> (This refers to the one specific car in the garage.)

Unit 21: Connecting Words: *Before, After, When, Because*

A clause has a subject and a verb.

> *Example:* He lives in Montreal.

Some sentences have two or more clauses.

> *Example:* **First Clause**   **Second Clause**
> You can get a driver's license   when you are 16.
> (subject *you* + verb *can get*)   (subject *you* + verb *are*)

The words *before, after, when,* and *because* can connect clauses.

> *Examples:* Some people wash their hands before they eat.
> Many students get a job after they graduate.

A clause with *before, after, when,* or *because* can come at the beginning or at the end of the sentence. If the clause comes at the beginning, a comma separates it from the rest of the sentence.

> *Examples:* I drive a used car because a new car is too expensive.
> Because a new car is too expensive, I drive a used car.

In speaking, the structure *because* + subject + verb is a common way to answer a *Why* question. In writing, do not use the structure *because* + subject + verb alone; connect it to another clause.

> *Examples:* Why do you get up so early?
> Because I work at 5:30 a.m.
> (OK in speaking but not in formal writing)
>
> I get up early because I start work at 5:30 a.m.
> (OK for both speaking and writing)

The words *before* and *after* can be prepositions followed by nouns.

>   *Examples:* Before class, I talked to the teacher.
>
>   After class, we often have some coffee.

Note the use of present-tense verbs in clauses about the future:

when/before/after + subject + present-tense verb,

subject + future verb

(or)

subject + future verb

+ *when/before/after* + subject + present-tense verb

>   *Examples:* Next year, after I get a job, I am going to buy a house.
>
>   Tomorrow, we're going to go shopping before we have dinner.

Unit 22: Past Progressive Tense

Past progressive verb forms: *was/were* + (verb + *-ing*)

>   *Examples:* He was studying.
>
>   Were you playing tennis?
>
>   They were not living in the capital.

The past progressive tense is used for actions that were continuous in the past or actions that took place over time in the past.

>   *Examples:* While she was smoking, I left the room.
>
>   We did not go to the beach yesterday because it was raining.
>
>   At 10:00 last night, we were watching a movie on TV.
>
>   She was studying when the phone rang.

The past progressive is often used with the connecting word *while*. When *while* begins the sentence, or interrupts it, use a comma between the *while* clause and the rest of the sentence.

>   *Examples:* While I was eating dinner last night, my friend called me.
>
>   John heard a noise last night while he was sleeping.
>
>   While my father was cooking dinner, my mother was reading.